GAME ON

*Reinventing Organizational Culture
with Gamification*

ARTHUR CARMAZZI

Acknowledgment

Special thanks to Dr Marshall Goldsmith who supported and inspired me to initiate this book. Marshall has been a great mentor and I owe him much of my success.

To my Kids, Dante and Alessandro Carmazzi, who helped me to begin the journey of structuring Gamification for emotional gratification to boring stuff when we applied it to them writing their first books at ages 7 and 10 and continue to inspire and teach me every day.

To my sweet wife Budi, who has always been my rock and foundation for creating my dream life.

Illustrations and graphics by: **FERI PRAYOGA**

Contributors:

Dr Marshall Goldsmith
New York Time Bestselling author of MOJO and What Got You Here Won't Get You There

Dr Sanjeev Dixit
Global HR Leader and acclaimed author of culture transformation book "PLAN C"

Rhiannon Rees
#1 business and Performance Coach in the US, 2019 #6 Global Coaching Guru.

Editors:

Bob Mittelsdorf

Joanne Ng

Dr Sanjeev Dixit

ABOUT THE AUTHOR

Arthur is ranked as one of the world's Top 10 most influential thought leaders in leadership and organizational culture by Global Gurus. As a bestselling author and founder of the Directive Communication Psychology, Arthur's gamification methodologies have influenced the training and leadership development industry through his unique game-based psychological approaches to leadership and corporate culture transformation. His innovative tools, assessments, and games, (including a game that helps organizations gamify work processes) have a visible ROI on engagement, productivity and effective behaviour modification. His research on the genetic foundations of the brain's Ambiguity Relief clarity getting processes have been the inspiration of the Colored Brain model used across multinationals in 57 countries. With over 540 licensed Directive Communication (DC) Psychology leadership and culture trainers in 19 different countries, DC is now a global brand.

Websites:

https://carmazzi.net (business website)

https://coloredbrain.com (team synergy system)

https://cultureevolution.com (culture benchmarking tool)

https://squadli.com (behavior gamification app)

https://emotionaldrive.net (Management perception gap analysis)

Social Links:

https://www.linkedin.com/in/arthurcarmazzi

https://twitter.com/Arthur_Carmazzi

https://www.facebook.com/Leadership.Speaker

https://plus.google.com/u/1/+ArthurCarmazzi

https://youtube.com/CarmazziTV

CONTENTS

Foreword by Marshall Goldsmith

My mission is to help successful people achieve positive, lasting change in behavior; for themselves, their people, and their teams. Coaching has been one of my processes of choice and I have been very successful at it. But there is another level. One of organizational culture. A level where a properly structured system can help more people to be successful and nurture positive lasting change in behavior across an entire organization.

This book is a guide, a fun one, to do just that. The reinvention of organizational culture to build positive lasting change where people enjoy work, find meaning and purpose in work, and support others to do the same. But GAME ON, takes it a step further so that we not only cultivate a happier more productive work environment but also a fun one. Arthur's proven psychology-based strategies and systems are laid out in a fun and easy to apply style to help create positive change across the organization.

Imagine that it's Monday morning and you are excited to get to work because you have some new ideas that will help you increase the numbers by the end of the month. You arrive, your team is eager to listen and start the ball rolling but you need cooperation from 2 other departments before you can start, you make a few calls and follow up with email and you have approval and full support within an hour. The excitement builds and the other departments are now also invested in your results so new excitement is distributed across departments. Because cooperation has become so easy, there is very little wasted time and each department and team member can focus on personal, team, and organizational achievement.

Sound unrealistic? Not with the strategies you will learn in this book. We are in a new age where people's emotional investments and expectations are very different than they used to be, and what used to work, may not be as effective now. Remember, what got you here, won't get you there.

Enjoy the book!

Life is good.

Marshall

We have experienced the evolution of human motivation first-hand and I have documented its transformations, consequences, and advantages in the infographic below. We have identified patterns in psychological models and created systems to harness the potential people can offer in their jobs and business. While today, the emotional gratifications are not different than 30 years ago, the expectations, speed, and process of achieving emotional gratification have drastically changed.

Download the Infographic at:
GameOn.management/graphic

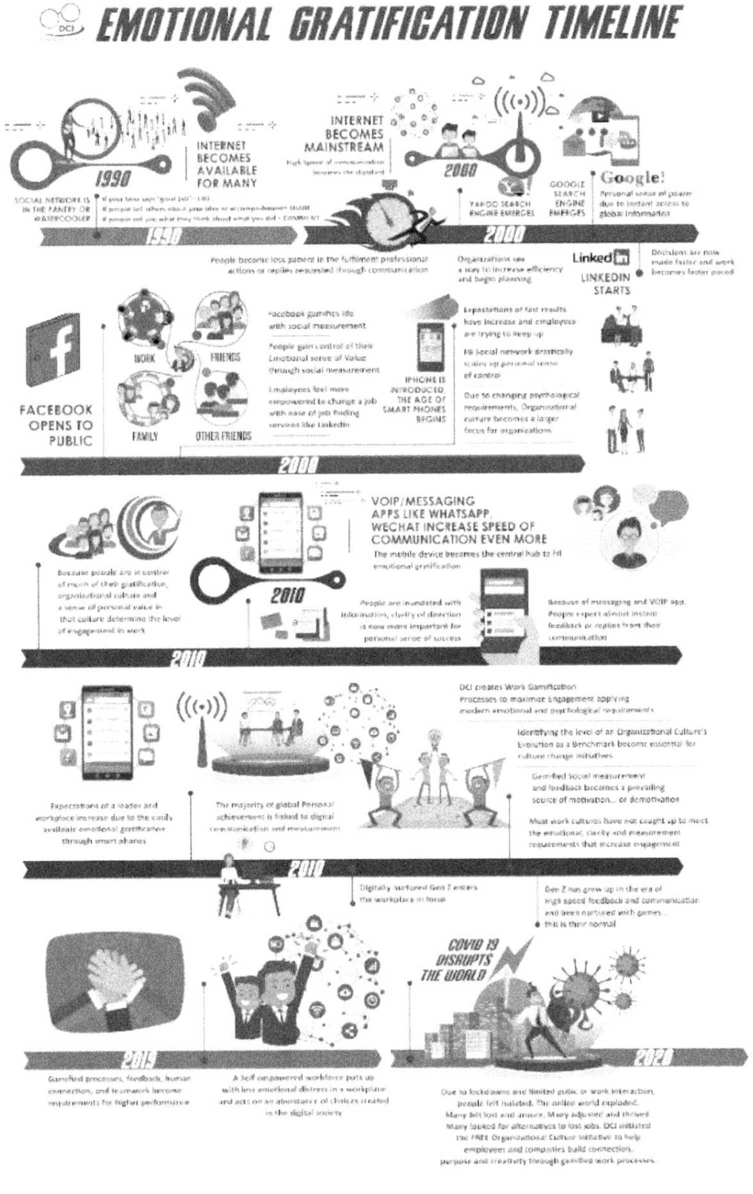

Setting Up the Gameboard of The New Organizational Culture Objective

Work gamification is about positive motivation structures triggering and maintaining excitement and interest in applying personal talents and innovation for the achievement of organizational goals…and for people to enjoy it.

Throughout this book, we will discover the elements, psychology, and strategies (plus look at multiple case studies) to create a culture of excited and engaged individuals who gain pleasure from achieving higher results. Yet, most employees have already achieved similar attitudes and engagement and then lost it.

We sometimes forget to start at the beginning. And when I say beginning, I mean the first few weeks of work at your new company. Do you remember how excited you were? The possibilities, the plans, the POTENTIAL!?! It was like, "WOW, it's Monday… I got to go to work today!!!" The future was bright and the potential for achievement and making a big impact in the organization was obvious. Everything you ever dreamed of in a job was possible… you just had to make it happen and you knew you had the potential, the value to add, and the new perspectives that would make all the difference.

But now, those dreams, that passion, the potential seems to have been misplaced and every now and then we find some of it, but the power is replaced by mediocrity. We are no longer this passionate powerhouse of 100% potential, we are less. We have become underachievers, not because our competency has reduced, or even that our potential to learn and develop has dwindled, but because the culture no longer supports our full potential.

I was one of these underachievers.

After getting into almost half a million dollars in debt] from failing in my own business, I needed to get a job... and I landed one, a good one. I was the head of product development for a large manufacturer in the stationary industry. The pay was good, and the future prospects were great... for a short time at least. After a while, I noticed that most everyone was blaming most everyone else for why things went wrong or even how they approached things. The marketing guys were blaming the finance department, the sales guys were blaming the R&D department, employees blamed HR, HR blamed the finance department. Come to think of it, everyone blamed finance at one point or another. I remember thinking to myself, "What is wrong with these people?"

But I knew in my heart I was an achiever, regardless of my previous failures, and I knew I could make an impact... so I came up with innovative ideas to improve the organization and the synergy across departments. But when I would bring up my ideas to the other departments, I got responses like: "We understand you are new here, but we are very busy with our own projects," and, "You do your thing, and we will do ours." There was no cooperation! I was disappointed, "How could they not see the bigger picture?" I thought.

I was frustrated, but I didn't give up, I knew I could make an impact... then, four and a half months later, without even realizing it... I started blaming people! Yes, including the finance department. People from other departments would come to me for help and I would tell them I was busy with my own things... "You do your thing and we'll do our thing..." I had gotten sucked in, I was now a part of the dysfunctional culture. But that wasn't the worst part... I had given up! All the ideas, the passion to do great things, the plans for the future were replaced by the need to "Get By". I didn't want to take the risk of being blamed, so [bm6] I waited for my boss to tell me what to do instead of being proactive. My innovative ideas became my secrets because I didn't want to go through more rounds of potential rejection. I felt stuck in my job, I had lost purpose, passion, and the motivation to excel. I had become mediocre! I had become an underachiever!

Only after almost a year of wallowing in my self-pity, did I wake up. I decided to talk to those "bad" people, those who didn't understand me, trust me, and who were making my life miserable, and I discovered something unexpected, they were real human beings, they also wanted to do something great, had aspirations of success that were pounded out of them, and they too had given up... they were just like me. This was the turning point for me which led to my research on organizational culture dynamics and the formulation of what would later become known as the Directive Communication Psychology... but that is another story.

When potential dwindles so does an organization's investment. If we are paying $5, 000 a month for a team member who has become 21% less effective* due to lower engagement, we are now getting $4,000 worth of value... but wait, there's more! What about the impact on the team and the team members themselves? That increase in apathy or reduced motivation has a continuous and profound effect on the entire team. And the team member is also affected... and not only at work, it can affect much of an individual's life. Have you ever had the feeling you could do more, be more, and yet, you felt stuck? A sense of being "stuck" affects your relationships in and out of work creating dysfunction in families and companies.

James K. Harter, Ph.D., Gallup's Chief Scientist and co-author of 12: The Elements of Great Managing shared that:

> *There's a significant relationship between work, stress, and health. In other words, if people are in an ongoing work situation that is negative or stressful, they have a higher potential for negative health consequences."*

Another key motivational factor is "Feeling" valued. The foundation of feeling valued however goes beyond one's individual manager and extends to the organizational culture. When the culture supports the opportunity for a team member to See, Feel, and Measure the "value" they add to a Bigger Organizational Goal, that culture will be more engaging and more efficient. Unfortunately, there are lots of barriers to overcome to do this.

According to a survey by the American Psychological Association (APA)

Feeling valued is a key indicator of job performance. Employees who feel valued are more likely to be engaged in their work and feel satisfied and motivated.

The Queen's School of Business research shows that disengaged workers had 37% higher absenteeism, 49% more accidents, and 60% more errors and defects. And the bottom line still stands out with engaged employees who outperform those without engagement by 202% according to a Gallup survey. Engagement is directly related to a personal sense of Value.

This stems from an organizational culture that does not have the emotional and structural elements to create environments that support engagement and innovation, and the development of the leaders to nurture and maintain those environments.

But where do we start to change this culture dynamic? Just like any game, you need to know where you are before you can begin your journey. The first step is to benchmark the culture. The biggest issue with benchmarking is the difference in perception from Senior Management, Middle Management, and Below Middle Management, so when decisions affecting the future of the organization are made, usually by senior management, they are biased to a culture that is usually a little rosier than the reality according to the other groups. More on culture benchmarking at: www.cultureevolution.com

We need a starting point where we require an honest look at what is really going on.

The Case of ALAN MULALLY and FORD by Marshall Goldsmith

When Alan assumed the role of CEO in 2006, here are a few of the top line "opportunities" that awaited him:

- Ford had just posted the largest annual loss in its 103-year history

- Stock was trading at $1 per share

- Employees were paralyzed with fear

Alan's first acts were to form a cohesive leadership team and to come together around a compelling vision, comprehensive strategy and relentless implementation process. He then convened a weekly meeting with the 16 members of his leadership team (all of whom would certainly qualify as credentialed Knowledge Workers). Initially, Alan asked each of them to do two things:

1. Identify a plan to implement the strategy.

2. Assess progress against the plan using the following guidelines:

GREEN| On plan. Currently on target and projected to achieve a goal.

YELLOW| Not currently on plan, but trending in a direction that would ultimately deliver desired results.

RED| Not on plan, and not sure how to get there.

The results from that first meeting? Each of the 16 team members reported GREEN (even though the company they ran happened to be in a tailspin headed toward a record $17 billion loss!). Considering the impending reality, Alan encouraged his team, "Let's do it again." After a period of time, Mark Fields (current CEO of Ford) finally said, "RED!" He then went on to candidly describe a problem of significance with no real strategy to fix it.

Looking back, Alan viewed this as one of the most important moments in the turnaround of Ford. In response to Mark's transparent assessment, Alan literally stood up and applauded. He congratulated Mark on having the courage to openly admit he had a problem – and even more – to admit that he had no idea on how to solve it, but that he was working on it.

He then said something few leaders have the nerve to say in the presence of their leadership teams:

"Mark, you have a RED.' Above all else, sincere thanks for the transparency! Also, please recognize this … it's OK! Now, just to be clear, I don't have the answer to your problem either. But, good news! We have thousands of very smart people who work here at Ford. Let's get to work and find somebody who can help Mark solve this problem."

What happened? The team turned their attention to Mark's problem and identified people who had the experience and expertise to help. Within a few minutes, there was noticeable movement in a positive direction. What followed were a series of bold and effective decisions that drove a truly legendary transformation. Alan retired in 2013 and during that year, Ford earned $7.2 billion, which translated to record profit-sharing bonuses of approximately $9,000 per employee

If we do not acknowledge the issues in our organization and our organizational culture, we can never facilitate improvement.

How the PFB (Post Facebook) era has Changed the Game Rules

As a speaker and consultant I understand that social media is an important part of marketing. And even though I have studied the biochemistry behind social media addiction, and I am fully aware of how and why it gets you hooked... I also find myself getting my emotional gratifications by checking my status and the number of social interactions across my social posting. I too have become a child (I use this term loosely) of the PFB era.

The PFB era is the age of "instant". Instant messages, instant information, instant visuals, even instant friends... but most importantly, instant emotional gratification! Our "social network" used to be at the water cooler or pantry. We would connect with our "friends" and verbally "post" (or complain) about what was going on in our lives. If people gave positive responses to our interaction, that was equivalent to a "Like", if they commented on the share, well, it was a "Comment". And if they told others about it, that was a "share". But all this has changed in this new era. We are now in control of the power of instant gratification through our Smart devices. Our expectations have changed, and so have our actions and reactions across all generations and cultures.

The measurement of social approval has always been the foundation of a personal sense of value, and in this PFB era, it has been digitized and supercharged. Everyone now has Power and a Voice. We are no longer emotionally dependent on our boss telling us we did a good job. If we feel we deserve more, we post ideas, occurrences, and humor online to get approval from our peers to compensate and recover emotional gratification.

Having more control over our emotional gratification creates an environment where we are less patient and have higher expectations of leaders and peers.

Communication is also related to patience and our emotional drive of Achievement. Achievement is not about completing something big, it is simply about completing something! The faster the communication, the more "Achievement" gratification we will potentially collect. This is why we start to freak out when someone doesn't reply to our messages or emails quickly. When we do not have the information or consent to make progress, our emotional gratification for achievement is delayed. And because it is delayed, we get frustrated, creating conflict, mistrust and more frustration in our teams. This is why longer projects that do not see results quickly, have the highest percentage of disengagement and procrastination.

Each generation approaches this differently but each is equally susceptible to its effects: [bm18]

> **Baby Boomers:** Still remember getting and sending letters (the paper kind), picking up the phone when it was an urgent matter and dealing with the speed of the local postal service. While the expectations in speed in our current age do not differ from any others, they are often more patient and communicative, ready to solve problems if they arise.

> **Gen X:** Computing started around the same time they were born; they were there during the evolution of the computer

and even learned computing in school. This generation evolved with the computer and easily adapted as it developed. This led to more flexibility and patience with leaders and as leaders. They are still susceptible to the current need for speed but tend to be more proactive if something is not as fast as it should be.

Gen Y (Millennials): Tend to be less patient but do communicate well. This generation takes more risk to fill their emotional drives and gratifications. Technology has played a part at home and at school. This group is more ready to give up and move on if things are not as fast as it should be, or the leaders are not in line with their higher expectations. The sense of entitlement this generation has been synonymously associated with is based on the need to feel special (the emotional drive of recognition) and achieve more (the emotional drive of achievement) ... thus so many start-ups and job changes.

Gen Z (iGen): This group gets most of its emotional gratification online. Since they get fulfillment through social media, they are more patient with real people who may not support their emotional drives, but the same factor reduces their potential to take risks, especially in communicating with others. These difficulties in communicating face to face are a product of more interaction online with the online image being more central to their gratification than their personal image. The expectations from a leader need to compete with this gratification so the standards are high. This generation has no problem working hard and earning recognition but will check out your social profile first and expect speed in online communication since this is all they have known.

The mechanics of social addiction.

Whether it's Instagram (the current favorite), Facebook, LinkedIn, or even Twitter, we are consistently checking our favorite platforms for 3 primary reasons.

1. We are looking for emotional fulfillment... it could be inspiration, humor, or simply the feeling of being connected to others.

2. We want to control and manage the impression we make on others. Our personal sense of security is connected to how much control we have over our lives. The "Impression" we make on others largely affects instinctual survival instincts that support belonging to a tribe.

3. We want validation of our lives – while this is also an emotional gratification, it's more complex than the word "Validation" can describe since it encompasses the previous two points.

    a. Many also use social media for businesses... but we still check the interactions of our efforts to either validate or adjust our strategy

    b. With the business focus, the emotional connection is even stronger for the "Win State", which is defined by the achievement of predefined business objectives.

So what does "Validation" mean?

When we post, we are posting elements of our life, our business, and our personal interests based on our emotional drives. We may post inspirational quotes so we feel like we are helping others find more light in their lives... or we may post them just to get visibility for our business. We may post pictures of our kids to show our pride in their development... or we may post them to keep our archive of their lives. We may post images of our travels to "show off" our lifestyle, or to share moments of discovery... but no matter what we post, most of us have one basic thing in common: we check to see how many likes, shares and comments we have.

These validation factors are a way for us to measure our personal sense of value (based on our current emotions). Regardless of how much self-confidence we have, or how much or how little we care about what people think. Since value is connected to purpose, if we feel valuable, we feel like our lives have more purpose... which creates more "happiness", at least for a moment!

This need to have a purpose (have value) stems from our ancient roots as tribal beings. Being valuable was required for our survival. If a member of a tribe did not add value to the tribe, they were left behind. So providing value to our "group" is directly related to our survival instinct and is a primal instinct, and being part of a tribe is directly related to safety, finding a mate and finding food.

And it can become an addiction not dissimilar to drug addiction since in essence, we are getting our Brain Drugs from it.

The brain produces these "drugs" to support our survival and help us make the right decisions to continue the human species...

One of these is the brain's social and reward center which includes, the Ventral Medial Prefrontal Cortex, the Ventral Striatum, and the Ventral Tegmental Area.

And the other is the brain's Reward Pathway which includes the *Striatum*, the *Nucleus Accumbens* and the *Amygdala* (two areas heavily associated with addiction). The Nucleus Accumbens is where mesolimbic dopamine is released (happy drugs among other things) and starts reward-seeking behavior (like checking and chasing Likes...). The Amygdala links environmental cues to reward and habit formation which basically associates your Social media success to Feel Good rewards and gets you hooked on the instant gratification these rewards provide.

But let's not forget the "Tribal Drugs" from connecting with people. These give us oxytocin (love and trust drugs) that not only reduce stress but can also support making us feel safe. Of course, this can backfire if you find pictures of your friends enjoying a party you were not invited to, or see an image of your friend's hot new partner when you just broke up with yours... but posting photos or videos (even food) makes you feel better if you are lonely. After all, you are sharing with others... and hopefully, they will LIKE you.

And those funny videos you watch or pictures of cats doing silly things... yup, more drugs. These are endorphins that are released when you laugh. Endorphins basically are pain reducers (including stress) and give you positive feelings similar to morphine.

Now whether social media is bad or good is not an argument for this book... but how and why is creating positive feelings, addictive behavior, and lessons from its negative effects are essential to creating positive gamification in our lives and work.

Technology vs. Humanity

Chapter introduction by Dr Sanjeev Dixit

Seasong HR Director in large Multi-nationals and Bestselling author of Plan C

*E*very new era brings its unique challenges and opportunities and the ongoing super technology revolution is posing a new level of growth dimensions to the Human race. It is not necessarily a battle between Technology & Humanity but it is an interesting synergy between the best features of both. This synergy is on setting a new phase of **Human-Technology** wherein Technology is enabling different levels of Cognitive and Emotional experience to Human further evolving their faculties and sensibilities. Just look at the entire impact of **Virtual Reality (VR)** in the way all the knowledge industries and consumers have accentuated their experience through real gamification. It has made the experience much more engaging, exhilarating, assimilating and enriching.

I believe Technology and Humanity will continue to complement each other by way of supporting the larger objective of enhanced experience humans want to achieve through technology. This complementary relationship is the fountainhead of all the NextGen innovation and creation in the field of Gamification. The only challenge area in this Gamification Universe would be to ensure Hi-Touch in the Hi-Tech environment and achieve personalized connect in an impersonal gamified world. Gamification is a huge boon for enabling high impact learning in low stake situations and such relevant learning yield long-

lasting impact on the business.

The battle begins. The Power of Technology against the ingenuity and emotiveness of Humanity. Let the games begin: There can only be one winner... or can there?

I have never been much of a gamer. The idea of using my time staring at a screen for an activity that would not provide any tangible result was difficult for me to fathom. But I was not and am not immune to the attractions of Game State... the emotional need to win, to overcome obstacles, to advance, to see visible improvement and even to "play" with others. I apply this in most areas across my life: My relationships, my work, parenting, and yes, play!

It is the common misbelief that gamification means apps or online games that require technology to achieve a "Game State". While technology can help, it can also distract us from the primary objective... Having Fun at Work, synergizing and bringing out the best in the "people" around us, and actually achieve objectives!

In most organizations, Teamwork is essential to achieve larger objectives. This teamwork extends beyond a project team to departments and the synergy between departments to achieve common goals. Getting people to communicate through apps, will not likely strengthen personal human relationships, plus the fact that empathy and human connection are required to create healthy teamwork.

Let's look at Planning. Have you ever planned a vacation? The process of planning provided anticipation of what was to come, each activity or even hotel you looked at and booked in advance created some excitement of what was to come. Our brain does not differentiate between planning a vacation, brainstorming about an idea you have to improve profitability or the excitement of what happens next in a game of candy crush. A neurotransmitter called Dopamine is released providing the "anticipation" of pleasure, and you don't need an app for that.

To get your dopamine fix (at least one of the five types that induce this anticipation of pleasure) and feel excited (increasing neuron firing rate) at work there are 8 fundamental elements that must be in place.

1. There must be an objective with a defined result

2. The result must apparently clear

3. You must believe the result will benefit you

4. You must believe you can achieve the result

5. The process to achieve the result should be in line with your primary motivators

6. You must be involved in the design of the process

7. The process should not be counter to your elemental genetic "Ambiguity Relief" process.

8. There must be clearly defined milestones that can be easily identified and measured when you achieve them.

9. There must have a backup plan or at least the feeling that

you have one

There must be an objective with a defined result

While this appears to be straightforward, we often forget to define what the result looks like. If we are relating our objectives directly to sales and revenue, it is pretty straightforward... but what if we want to be better leaders, or improve cross-departmental communication? The objective may be improving X by Y% or Z number, but the result is what it looks like. How do people feel? What are the effects on other areas when the objective is met? What will it do for retention or absenteeism? Is it something people can visualize? How will I personally be affected by the achievement of the result?

The result must apparently clear

This is about how this is communicated. Are you using examples everyone can understand? Is there an infographic? Do you have a before and after video? Are you using common words and phrases to assure the understanding of all involved? Is it laid out in a flowchart or mind map?

You must believe the result will benefit you

While this idea is often related to incentives (often trips or money), the incentive can be emotional gratification like recognition, or the "potential" of being more or achieving more. As is defined in the next chapter, there are 8 fundamental motivators that we fill through various actions and inactions. We must feel that there will be a personal reward if we achieve the result

The process to achieve the result should be in line with your primary motivators

Since Gamification is directly related to our primary motivators, the game process must be designed to provide a variety of emotional gratifications to ensure they trigger multiple individuals Primary Motivators. Emotions that one may cherish, others may not, so we must design a game process to fill multiple emotional gratifications in the course of achieving objectives.

You must be involved in the design of the process

The anticipation of achievement is the addictive part of the work and the foundation of engagement. When we are involved in the design process, we begin to see the potential and create that anticipation of what is possible. This supports excitement that will get even more committed to the work gamification process that is created.

The process should not be counter to your elemental genetic "Ambiguity Relief" process.

Our brain's clarity getting process has its foundations in genetics. This is called the Ambiguity Relief process. How we get clarity has strong foundations in how we develop trust and feel respected in groups since what may seem like "common sense" to others, may not be common sense to us... potentially creating opportunities to be misunderstood. If a gamification process is counter to our own clarity developing process, we tend to be out of alignment with it and may feel it doesn't "fit" which leads to disengagement. To overcome this barrier, we incorporate elements from the 4 primary Ambiguity relief processes as described through the Colored Brain. This will enable multiple individuals with multiple processes to trust the system and believe it will have an impact. More detail on this in Chapter 5.

There must be clearly defined milestones that can be easily identified and measured when you achieve them.

Milestones are the foundation of anticipation. Each milestone triggers the emotional gratification of achievement and shows progress toward a bigger goal. This progress reinforces that the actions you are taking are working and generate more excitement and motivation to continue. For this to be most effective, milestones need to be achieved quickly. If you can achieve a milestone every 2 or 3 days, you maintain the motivation momentum about winning over another, it is about the specifics related to measurement.

There must have a backup plan or at least the feeling that you have one

The fear of failure can be a big barrier to confidence so a backup plan not only mitigates the risk of failure, but it provides the additional confidence that will help you start and keep you going.

When we add these 8 elements to the 3 gamification criteria, we are able to create Human Structures that support engaged thinking, innovation and action toward the defined objectives. The 3 criteria:

1. Measurement

2. Competition

3. Story or theme

Measurement

While performance measurement apps like "Squadli" come in handy for instant feedback, measurement takes on a greater role (discussed in detail in chapter 6). It is key to how we feel when we know how we are doing. The biggest issue has always been about how to keep everyone motivated when often, it is only 3 or 4 people who hog the top spots… Fortunately, there are a number of practical solutions depending on the types of teams you have… explained in Chapter 6. Remember to keep feedback Objective.

Competition

Competition is usually assumed to be with others but that is not required in work gamification… You can compete against a previous score or percentile. You can compete against another team. You can compete against an industry standard. You can compete against the amount of time it takes to achieve a specific goal…

Story or theme

Every addictive game has a story or a theme. Bringing our reality to a different realm. This supports our emotional drive for Diversity. Diversity is at the core of "Fun". Solving a problem at work with your team could become mundane. But if we are solving the same problem with an elite team of international spies in order to save the world from an evil warlord, somehow, it's just more fun, which translates to more engagement. And when Diversity is combined with other emotional drives such as Belonging, Growth, Recognition, and/or Achievement, the addition of motivators increases the engagement. This is why for some, it's fun to go to the mall with friends even if you are not planning to buy anything. More on this in chapter 4.

When technology improves humanity!

The premise of great leadership is to be able to bring out the best in others and nurture a culture that maintains that best. The human element is the foundation and that must be the center of the culture. Humanity in leadership and performance cannot be replaced by technology… but it can be supported. One of the difficulties in great leadership is the ability to both give instant feedback on performance (most importantly Positive Performance) and maintain an ongoing record of the performance. This is where technology comes in.

But this is where gamification strategy is essential because simply measuring and supporting performance can go VERY WRONG if not structured to enhance the sense of value across the entire team.

When we use technology with apps like Squadli to measure, record, and gamify performance, we connect our emotions and gratitude to the actions of others. Using these types of apps for ranking, awards, emoji, and applying it to instant feedback… can express and convey the Value we feel others bring to the group. This allows teammates to feel they are valuable and on the right track (or not). Without apps like this, the process becomes tedious and is usually short-lived…

The emotional equilibrium required to attain success can be identified through the **Gamification Value Perception Index** (GVPI). A measurement of the sense of value in relation to comparison and measuring contribution and the emotional states it creates.

As mentioned in the previous chapter, the emotional need to feel valuable is a prominent factor in successful gamification and goes back to our early tribal roots of survival. While the need to add value is instinctive, we never had to be the best or even in the top 20, so we became complacent in the levels of the value we were providing. As long as it was good enough, we were still ok. Perspective is largely related to our self-perception and confidence. Lower levels of confidence are directly related to lower levels of performance, or the attitude of performance.

	EMOTION OF FEELING UNVALUED	EMOTION OF FEELING VALUABLE
COMPARISON	**GIVE UP** Seldom achieve top rankings and feel they cannot be one of the best so they sink into mediocrity. They give up.	**STAY MOTIVATED** Achieve top ranking enough to feel they can be one of the best and are constantly striving to stay or achieve these ranks
MEASUREMENT OF CONTRIBUTION	**LOW CONFIDENCE** Not getting enough timely/quick positive feedback or getting negative feedback without a direction or opportunity to improve and be acknowledged for it	**GROWTH** Getting fast positive feedback on contribution to organization and bigger goals. When receiving negative feedback, clear directions to achieve higher levels of performance

Gamification Value Perception Index

Why? Because of comparison, we usually compare ourselves to the high performers, and when it seems we can not compete, we often settle into complacency, unless we find another area we can excel in.

Long ago I dated a rather pretty girl from Singapore. She was highly intelligent but looking back she did have some self-esteem issues. I recall one instance where we were looking at an airline magazine and came across an ad of an extremely seductive model showing a particular brand of perfume, the implication was that if you use this, you would be super sexy too. But that was not her focus. She wanted to know if she was as pretty as the model in the magazine. And in my desire to have a totally honest and transparent relationship, I told her the truth… and it wasn't what she wanted to hear! This was the beginning of the end for that relationship but it taught me an important lesson… we often compare ourselves to idealistic standards rather than to our strengths and personal improvements over time.

There will always be individuals who simply perform better overall than others but with gamification, we have an opportunity to improve lower performers' attitudes and performance with modern psychology. While it's great for already high performing individual's morals and sense of personal value to be high ranking, it could be destructive for others who have potential but not quite there yet. We, as emotional beings (yes, even if you are very logical and "feel" you make decisions logically), tend to require a balance of achievement AND potential to achieve.

Because we gravitate towards opportunities to practice our strengths, we tend to consistently improve those strengths. This can be harnessed for overall improvement through gamification. For example, if we are on the list of top performers in the area of "communication", that becomes "our thing" and we don't want to lose it. Even if we are not on the most important list, we feel like we are already providing value. The gap is smaller to the more important list and so we gain more motivation to get to that higher list.

If however, the gap is too large, we tend to compare to others who achieve some level of recognition and feel less valuable, creating lower motivation and we often disengage or even give up on trying to reach a higher level of achievement.

	POTENTIAL TO ACHIEVE	ACHIEVEMENT
COMPARISON	**ANTICIPATION** Being in the lower TOP of a comparison at least once provides the "Potential" to be in the top of the top more consistently… to be more and be recognised for it	**COMPLETION** Being in the Top of the TOP shows achievement, going lower is like taking away what you already have so we tend to maintain the commitment to prevent loss
MEASUREMENT OF CONTRIBUTION	**REINFORCE COMPETENCE** Reinforce competence through measurement or identify personalized strategies to become more competent and reinforce various levels on competence through points or status	**VALIDATION** Measurement validates achievement. Creating relevant awards or points and connecting achievements to specific large company objectives provides a greater sense of achievement and specific value

Gamification Value Perception Index

Having a specific and sincere acknowledgement of achievement leads to feelings of being of value in the organization.

Feeling there is Potential for higher achievement or progress of achievement creates motivation and engagement.

This means any gamification initiative must include multiple opportunities to succeed as well as the "feeling" that if you persist, you can achieve and succeed more and have more value. One means of achieving this is comparison. The ability to compare personal achievements, even small ones, to the potential of achieving higher levels of success. A comparison of an existing small success is much closer to bigger success than no success at all.

This type of comparison is subconsciously applied when we buy things. I found myself in a clothing store where they were having a "Buy 2 for sale". They had a nicely designed set of cargo pants at $120, but the sale was "Buy 2 at $180... my instinct was to buy 2 it didn't matter that I originally had no intention of buying anything, but it seemed like such a good deal. I would save 50% of the price for the 2nd pair (or $60). Without even realizing it, I bought 2 pairs of the same color because I compared the gap between the original price of the pants to the sale price of the second pair. It felt like I was saving $60. I rationally knew that it was only a saving of $30 per pair when I bought two, but the focus and justification were based on the comparison to the 50% off of the second pair... and yes, I felt successful that I had achieved such a great deal!

It is important to note that not everyone likes the "idea" of work gamification, but emotional gratifications are still factors in their motivation. So gamification processes still have positive effects on people who feel that work should be serious as long as each person "feels" that they are adding value.

Additionally, not all people are driven by recognition, so gamification elements of supporting the idea that one is valuable, cannot only be related to being publicly recognized for that value. And this is where the Gamification journey comes in.

The index is ideal in the harmony between technology and humanity because it addresses variables essential for motivation in both areas.

Anticipation: ranking can support anticipation of performers who have potential but are not at their achieving it. Using apps that create ranking is useful here. Leader boards for different levels of achievement can also be applied but become more labor-intensive.

Developing Competence & Engagement through Gamification

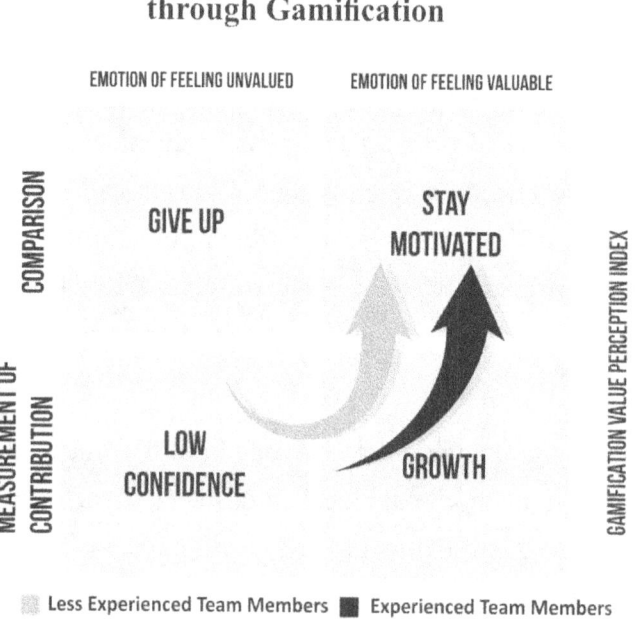

EMOTION OF FEELING UNVALUED   EMOTION OF FEELING VALUABLE

COMPARISON

GIVE UP

STAY MOTIVATED

MEASUREMENT OF CONTRIBUTION

LOW CONFIDENCE

GROWTH

GAMIFICATION VALUE PERCEPTION INDEX

Less Experienced Team Members ■ Experienced Team Members

Validation: measurement and awards support validation of value. But specificity is essential since the value is directly related to the associations of personal actions and behaviors that were responsible for the results. This is why apps like Squadli that connect the specificity and measurement with instant feedback are useful.

Entering the realm of The Psychology of FUN

You're standing at the gates. The anticipation of a day of adventure, excitement and new experiences awaits. You have an idea but there is still so much new experience to look forward to. You open your eyes, the gates to the realm of fun are in your imagination. The emotions are not in the result, but in the process of experiencing the unknown

My family and I went on a ski vacation to the Swiss Alps. Living in Bali, snow is something we don/t see, not even at the top of the volcano. In fact, I was not just the only one of us who could ski, I was the only one who had experienced snow. My sons, Dante and Alessandro (age 10 and 7) couldn't wait to start skiing, my wife was wearing her new ski outfit and was ready to test it out on the slopes. We chose the Vercorin because it was one of the easier resorts, and I wanted to make sure everyone was safe. I was the leader... Father will get everyone skiing by the end of the day and it will be so much fun... until we get to the midpoint of the mountain. It was snowing and windy! Not the best ski weather in my experience. As we stepped out into this weather I felt that I may disappoint my family and that it would not be as fun as I had anticipated. But that's not what happened, the snow, the cold, the wind were all new experiences. Everyone was just excited to be there. My wife was satisfied that her outfit was keeping her warm and everyone was simply having fun just seeing and experiencing the snow. But as the leader, I needed to make sure we achieved the result, to get everyone skiing. This was the beginning of the end of the fun... there is a fine line between fun and fear, they are both connected to the same emotion... but first, what is fun?

Why do we "Have Fun" when we go to a game or go shopping with our friends? Why do we enjoy travel or sports? Why is buying something new fun? …and why is it more fun if we are buying stuff with friends or family? …what do all these have in common?

Before entering the psychology of Fun, we must prepare for our journey, an understanding of our "Emotional Drive" will pave the road to awareness and show the origin of how fun emerges.

Emotional Drive is a set of primary motivators that may change as our life changes. We tend to be more motivated to fill some than we are to fill others. There are usually a top 3 or 4 that influence most of our decisions. Yet those in the bottom 2 or 3 are equally important since these are not highly motivating to us and we give those up to fill our primary drives.

There are eight Emotional Drives*, they are:

1.   The Drive for Diversity and Change: Different experiences, anticipation, and newness…

2.   The Drive for Love and Belonging: Being with people. Caring and being cared about

3.   The Drive for Recognition and Significance: To feel valuable. To be recognized by others and self as important or significant

4.   The Drive for Achievement: To complete things, to make progress on goals, achievement shows itself accomplishment of any size or type

5.	The Drive for Excellence: To do more than is expected or needed in order to make something better; a higher standard

6.	The Drive for Challenge and Growth: To become more than you already are, to improve oneself, to challenge your ability, and learn...

7.	The Drive for Contribution and Responsibility: A sense of responsibility for humanity. Giving selflessly for the betterment of other

8.	The Drive for Security and Control: Feeling safe, secure. Being in control of your life, your future

Out of Eight Emotional Drives, the one that defines if we have "fun" or not, is the drive for Diversity and Change... and the more of our other primary drives that combine with this, the more fun we have (or at least think we will have)

Fun comes from being OUT of the ordinary. When a situation is new, outside of our current day to day routine, we fill our emotional drive for Diversity and Change. This is largely affected by the feelings of anticipation that are created from a new, or at least out of the ordinary experience.

When we anticipate something, we generally have an expectation of what we will get, but we are not sure. This promotes a sense of adventure... and "Fun" is essentially an adventure in enjoying the process and anticipating what "Might" happens, in relation to the expectation. ...and even when we feel we do not have an expectation, we are "Expecting" to be surprised.

It is important to appreciate that fun is not elicited from an end result. It comes from The Process!

This is why "Work" can be "Fun" if staged in the proper settings and structured to deliver specific emotional gratifications. *These emotional gratifications needed to be unique and personalized through the kind of experience they will have on the way to achieve the objective while having fun.*

When I was building my house "Avalon", I found myself working with the masons, stone carvers, and woodworkers in my spare time. The work was often strenuous, but to me, it was fun...

1. It was out of the ordinary

2. It allowed me to be creative

3. It let me learn new things

4. I often involved my kids in the process

5. We were able to see progress as we worked on it

6. I felt I was doing "Man's Work" and that I am playing a part in the construction of my own house

7. It created new challenges I had not experienced before

8. It was part of a bigger vision that stemmed from childhood

Each of these elements was filling an emotional drive

- Out of the ordinary and creativity filled the drive of Diversity and Change

- The learning element of the experience filled my drive for Challenge and Growth

- Involving the kids was the drive for Love and Belonging

- Physically seeing our progress as we work was the drive for Achievement

- The sense of being more manly filled my drive for Recognition and Significance

- The Drive for Excellence: To build a masterpiece like Avalon which was out of comfort zone.

The Fear Tolerance Scale

How much diversity a person is willing to act on is subject to the importance or ranking of their emotional drive of Security and Control. The drive for Security defines the threshold between Fun and Fear. This is called the Fear Tolerance Scale. The more Security one needs, the lower the Fear Tolerance is. When we have the anticipation that something will have a neutral or positive outcome, fun is the result. But when that anticipation changes to a potentially negative outcome, the result is fear.

My dearest wife, Budi and I are complete opposites when it

comes to how much Security we need in our lives. I am a risk-taker while she is… well not! When we were on the slopes of Alps in Vercorin, my emotional drive for achievement was directly connected to getting my family to ski reasonably well. That was my objective and by god, it was going to happen. My determination that I would have a result in a single afternoon was tied to my drive for recognition, I would be the Hero once again to my family… Tan Tan Tan!

To achieve this, I thought teaching them the way I learned in university would be the best way… not taking into consideration the age of my children or the security focus of my wife, and so here we were in the middle of the mountain with skiers passing by us going down the main slope… The kids and Budi were stumbling with their skies as we huddled together to discuss the plan! "We are going to zig-zag to make sure we don't go too fast," I said. "…and we are going to point our skies at the front making a V" I continued. As I tried showing them my kids tripped over their skis and my wife just stood there, frozen with fear. "Are you trying to kill your family?" she resounded… "This is not the way to learn for kids and beginners!"

But my emotional drives for achievement and recognition far exceeded my tolerance of my wife's emotional drive for security and I persisted telling her it would be fine once they started. And so what started as a new and fun experience for my wife, turned into fear and a perspective that I was only interested in my own agenda. This led to anger and frustration… the fun was gone! Fortunately, a new hero emerged and overshadowed my lack of empathy. A ski instructor who saw the fear in my family and my lack of experience stepped up and suggested we move to a learning field that was at a different location. He even offered to give us a ride.

We took the tram back to the base and he met us at the bottom. The new location was barely challenging I felt, but my family was now feeling safe, and so the potential fun was reignited now that fear of death was no longer on the table. My drive for recognition had been deflated, I was no longer the hero. But now that the situation was compliant to a more secure process, Achievement and Love & Belonging were now my focus and the rest of the day was served to have more fun for everyone.

It is the emotional drive of Security & Control that creates the difference in the types and even the intensity of fun. Security turns the anticipation feeling of the Diversity drive into a potentially negative outcome thus creating fear. When the **Fear Tolerance** is less than the fulfillment of the Diversity drive combined with other drives, fun changes to fear.

The higher the need for Security, the more risk an action seems to have. And if diversity combined with other emotional drives requires risk, this action is limited to the amount of perceived risk it brings. Risk is defined by emotional and physical risks. The risk of being ridiculed is as potent as the risk of having a broken leg. So what may seem fun to a person with a low drive for Security may seem crazy for a person with high Security.

The fulfillment of the other emotional drives is affected too. Diversity combines with other drivers, the importance of the other drivers compared to Security determines the "types" of fun we like to have and when diversity turns to fear.

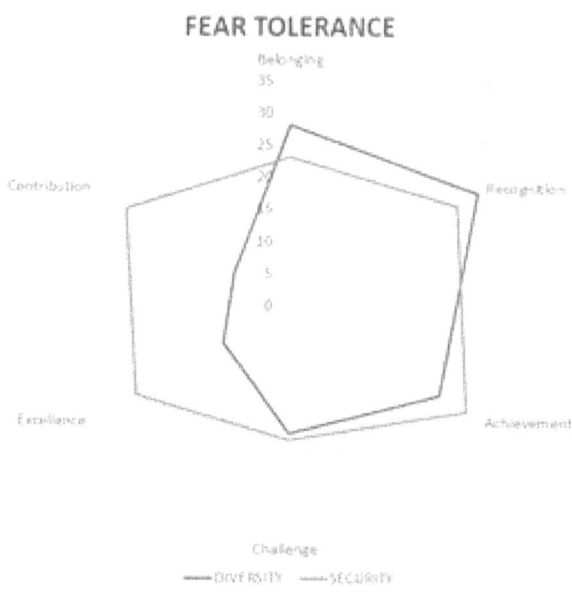

FEAR TOLERANCE

In this case, the Security drive is larger than the most other drives except the Belonging and Recognition drives. This indicates that this person's Fear Tolerance for only these two drives is slightly higher and they will take more risk to fill their drives of Recognition and Belonging through fun activities. Overall, their Fear Tolerance is low.

These activities can include going out with friends, showing you're doing something that shows others what you have done, dressing to stand out…

Challenge and Achievement are also very high so this person will do things they do not feel too risky to challenge their current ability, learn new things and make sure things get done. Because Belonging is important, this person may do things out of peer pressure... especially if it is connected to recognition.

This person will not be looked at as "FUN LOVING" and will most likely be considered to be more "Serious"

FEAR TOLERANCE

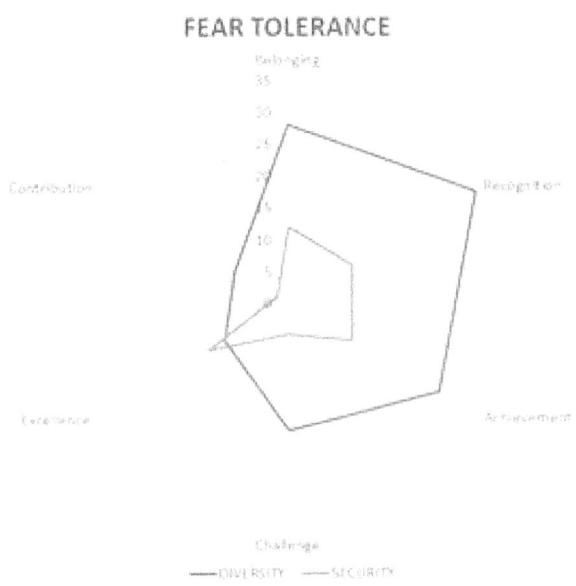

In this case, the Security drive is lower than most emotional drives except Excellence, and the gaps are larger. This means that this person is willing to take lots of risk to get fulfillment through Diversify for most of their drives. They have a very High Fear Tolerance.

The activities this person would have fun being ambitious as shown with the high diversity in Recognition and achievement.

They also prefer to work in teams or hang out with family or friends and enjoy learning and challenging activities... but will be more focused and stick to a specific standard when doing something that requires an added sense of excellence.

They will be considered a FUN LOVING person and seem to be able to have fun in most situations.

The enemies of fun are the enemies of engagement

But the emotional drive of Security & Control is not the only enemy of fun. The potential for fun can also be taken away when the circumstances or an environment take away the emotional drives that are important to you. Not only do you not have fun, but you become disengaged... ultimately leading to underachievement or simply maintaining the status quo.

We call this "Need Sucking" because it sucks away your emotional gratifications. While this is a common and possibly even daily occurrence in most of our lives, we often react to it as if it were a personal attack. It's not! Need sucking is usually the result of someone trying to fill their own emotional drives while accidentally sucking away yours.

Blaming others, for example, is usually the result of someone trying to recover their drive for Significance & Recognition and/or security. And if you are blamed, you react because it sucks away your drive for Recognition and possibly Security as well... and the cycle continues.

If you have 2 or more children, you will relate to them fighting over our perception of insignificant circumstances. My sons Dante and Alessandro often play with their Lego's. But what appears Insignificant to us as parents, is not to them in the balance of the creation of the perfect spaceship. The use of that one special Lego piece is far more important than you realize. The fun of building their Lego army together can immediately turn into a battle to preserve the potential drives of Achievement and Excellence derived from adding that one unique brick. And when that brick stands in the way of finishing their idea as the only way they envision it… Need Sucking is inevitable. The moment Dante wants a specific piece, Alessandro makes the realization that he needs that more than he does, the piece now represents a higher sense of Significance and Excellence connected to his drive for Achievement. Dante is now need sucked for Achievement, Excellence, and Significance causing him to react and the battle begins.

The battle for fulfillment has far more dire consequences than the right Lego for the job. In fact, "The Job" is the focus of so many investments in the development of engagement, innovation, and team synergy that are directly related to the emotional gratifications of individuals and how those motivations affect performance and organizational culture. The difference in an organization where adults are the players and the Lego brick is a resource or a coveted project… is that rather than deal with conflict, players often remain quiet but not forgiving or forgetful. Quietly making judgments, feeling underappreciated, perceiving a lack of respect and trust… which is manifested in lower innovation, performance, and engagement creating a pool of people with high potential who are motivated to be and act less than their potential. In other words, Need Sucking is one root cause for becoming an underachiever and the inevitable effects that it has on organizational culture... unless you know what's really happening.

Fear of conflict or rejection is not a new thing in organizations, but gamifying communication to resolve these before they transform your excitement to indifference is. In the next chapter, we will share how you can build trust, eliminate root causes that kill trust, and set a gamified foundation where language will translate to becoming more of who you want to and need to become.

* The 8 Emotional Drives are expanded from Anthony Robin's 6 human needs, Maslow's hierarchy of needs and our own perspectives based on research

Bonus round for climbing the Tower of Trust

Trust is the foundation of innovation, proactive action, and engagement. Without trust, we wait for instructions instead of taking initiative. We hold back our suggestions instead of sharing our potentially ground-breaking ideas. And if we feel that we cannot earn trust, we feel undervalued and therefore become underperformers.

In the previous chapter on Technology vs. Humanity, we discussed how we seek to validate our value, and how this is one of the foundations of positive motivation. One of the greatest validations is trust. Are you trusted to add value in the way you know you can, are you trusted to ask for help when you need the support, are you trusted to be accountable to working, supporting and implementing at your best…?

As important as we know trust is, many organizations unintentionally train their people out of trust. Trust requires an emotionally safe environment. One where we can express ourselves and be heard, where people focus on the objective, not the process, and one where mistakes are stepping stones to greater competence.

When management focuses on what has gone wrong and who's at fault rather than what the solution is and how can we can fix it, we tend to develop a fear of being wrong… which turns to limitations on trying anything new… which minimizes innovation… which makes us feel we are less valuable… which creates disengagement.

Because the managers have their own winning formula in approaching things, they may impose processes on us that we feel are, well, less than adequate... we feel they don't trust us and our perceived better way to approach our work.

So if we can build an environment of trust... being trusted and being able to trust others, everything else we do will work better, faster and easier.

After failing in business and getting a half a million dollars in debt, I needed to get a job.

It was 2nd week on the job. I was excited to be a part of this new and very large (and let's keep it nameless) organization... my sights were set on making a big impact, get noticed, get promoted and keep going to the top. As head of product development, I had already come up with one new idea and even a prototype. It was new, it was modern, and it was what the younger segments would pay more money for. I was eager to show it to my boss knowing that he would be impressed that I had been proactive and created something noteworthy in such a short time. I went into his office, explained it and the market segment it would apply to... and... he suggested that this was not our market and that anything high end was risky... and that I should focus on the same types of products we were already making... but possibly with different materials.

I felt disillusioned after all the CEO had hired me to be innovative, to bring some new ideas and a fresh perspective, but now my immediate boss was countering my entire purpose. But determined to show my boss what I could do, without going over his authority to the CEO, I decided to take the challenge and use existing products as a base. In my second presentation, my boss told me I was "Too Creative"... under normal circumstances that would be a compliment, but not this time!

Disillusioned once again, I thought I would bring it up to the CEO. A risky action but after all, I had a responsibility to do what I was hired for. And after our discussion the outcome was... that my boss was in charge and that he would not be a good leader if he undermined him. While I could understand the leadership decision, I could no longer see what value I was really bringing to the organization. I felt I was hired under false pretenses. So I asked my boss what he thought I should do and he told me it was my job... I felt stuck and unmotivated! I began to do the bare minimum and maintain the status quo, which seemed to please my boss. Life sucked!

I felt untrusted. If I tried my ideas, they were rejected. I needed to simply redress existing products to gain approval, a job I felt was better suited for an accountant rather than a creative one. I also didn't trust my boss and thought he was outdated. I felt betrayed by the CEO who I felt led me to believe my job was actually making an impact, but then it wasn't. I did try an occasional new idea, but they were rejected, so I just stopped... I started doing "Busy Work" to fill my time. As soon as it was 4pm, I started staring at the clock, I couldn't wait till the day ended... Fridays were great, and I dreaded Mondays. I had become an underachiever. I had become mediocre. I had no purpose.

Having a sense of purpose and value is essential to perform at your peak. But there is a greater enemy to trust that sneaks up on you without even realizing it. Blame!

When I first started the job I did notice how everyone blamed everyone else, it was a daily routine and I felt disgusted. How could these people maintain this toxic environment? Four and a half months later, I noticed that I was blaming others, in fact, I had become a Master Blamer and picked up the skill very fast. I had been sucked into behavior that I didn't approve of and outwardly rejected, yet here I was. At first, it was self-defense blaming, others would blame me then I would react by blaming them back or blaming the person who had some role in the issue... or the default if nothing came to mind, was blaming the finance or HR department, everyone blamed them.

Later I graduated to a proactive blamer, I would literally look for faults and problems in other department's work that would have any effect on my department's efficiency. I had now earned my "Destroy Trust" and "Create Silos" Merit badges, but it was all part of the environment... until I fully realized that I had become the type of person that I could not respect. So things needed to change.

I spent about 9 months trying to figure out why someone who is reasonably intelligent and has a disdain for this type of behavior (namely me), can become the person that is not in line with who they really are and react in ways that counter their own logic. In this chapter, I share some of the insights from that research and how we can use them to create an environment of trust then use gamification to keep it fun and sustainable.

Strategies for building an Environment of Trust

There are specific root causes of why trust breaks down. Here are some ways to fix them

Repositioning Fear Tolerance

The differences in Fear Tolerance levels are one of the most common trustbusters in teams, relationships, and even governments. This happens when one person has a high Fear Tolerance (FT), and another has a low one. Perceptions of the right amount of risk or even what is a risk and what is not, create scenarios where the actions surrounding the perception kill trust.

A person with a high FT will want and even expect others on a team to take action, innovate, be creative… but the person with the low FT will be more cautious and take more time. They may see the high FT person as reckless or uncaring. While the person with the high FT may feel that the low FT individual is dragging them down or cannot be trusted to make things happen. This difference in perception can create frustration and the frustration breeds low trust.

My clarity is not your clarity

Trust is a product of feeling safe, the absence of fear when interacting with others. But, when others do not understand us or try to push a process on us that we feel is not supporting our success, fear is ignited because we feel our ability to add values is reduced.

There are certain ways of doing things that seem like complete common sense to you. And you will meet intelligent people, who seem to completely ignore the rules of "common sense" when approaching a project or task. This is often frustrating and usually causes some form of reaction, perception or assumption that affects how you treat these people. Often, these effects can signal a lack of trust because they appear to discount the value the individual is offering. The disconnect of "common sense" is often directly related to how you get clarity. Your clarity process determines the progression and sequences related to action and what you require to feel comfortable in taking action.

How we get clarity determines how we approach a project, relationships, ideas, learning, or even define our emotions and personal values. Because our clarity getting process is often different than someone we may work, or have a relationship with, it is frequently the cause of misunderstanding, unintentional disrespect, and a source of distrust.

Based on the genetic brain research I began in 2002 and completed in 2017, there is conclusive evidence that your brain achieves clarity through a genetic process called Ambiguity Relief. This process is not a behavior or habit which can be affected by neuroplasticity, it is not personality… it is a specific way of "how" your brain makes connections and interprets information to make sense of the world.

Consider an iPhone which uses a Motorola processor, and an Android phone which uses an Intel processor. The apps they use can achieve the same result, but the physical way of processing differs. Each app must be specifically designed for a specific processor. You cannot take apps or even iOS made for a Motorola processor on an iPhone and run it on a Samsung phone. Our brain's processor runs in a similar way in that it is the hardware which is the platform for the software to work.

Remember when you went to school, some students appeared to get good grades in some classes without needing to study. While others who were also smart, needed to study a lot just to keep up. But the reason may not be that those students were smarter than you. Imagine the teacher wearing red-colored classes, everything they would interpret would be in a red way, they would design their curriculum in a red way, they would lecture in a red way and their tests and homework would be designed and graded in a red way. If a student is wearing the same red glasses, it would seem easy, common sense. But if they were wearing blue or green glasses, this would require interpretation, translation, study.

To make it easier to understand and apply this research, we have created a system to identify and measure the brain's ambiguity relief process, and connect team members so they can identify themselves, their colleagues and who is in their "Danger Zone". We made categories in the form of colors so we call this the "Colored Brain"

While I have written entire books *("The Colored Brain Communication Field Manual"*, and the *"Hero's Way – Finding the Colored Brain")* on Colored Brain and its implications on Team Synergy, Performance, Relationships, Leadership, and

Organizational Culture, the applications of Colored Brain to building trust is what we focus on in this book.

Trust starts with accepting that our process to get clarity is genetic. Which means it cannot be changed. It's like telling a brown-eyed person that you do not like brown eyes and that they should have blue eyes. Even if they run out and get blue eye contact lenses to try and please you, they still have brown eyes. Usually, when we judge people based on some genetic bias, we call this racism. When we judge people by the color of their brain, this is "Brain Racism"... The awareness that it is genetic and cannot be changed, helps non-racists to reduce the Brain Racism that most of us unwittingly engage in. I say brain racism because, without realizing it, we are judging and even diminishing the value of others due to their different brain process genetics. When we recognize we cannot change others, we tend to move on and work with what we have, allowing them to be free to be successful in their own way... even though it may seem alien to us.

When we know our own Ambiguity Relief clarity getting process, we can manage our expectations when dealing with others which provides a greater sense of control reducing the potential fear and increasing the potential for trust.

When we know other's processes, we can set them up for success instead of failure. We create an environment where people feel they are in control of the value they offer and feel trusted by you because you "understand" them and accept them and their potential.

This is not to say that education and training others is of little importance. The more awareness a person has, the easier it is for them to accept, ignore, or improve the ideas they receive.

Since action is the key to achievement, and clarity is the foundation of action, know the process of clarity is a powerful tool in not only developing trust but in creating more efficiency.

Here are the different Ambiguity Relief processes and their corresponding color:

Chaotic Processing (Green Brain)

1. Must take some kind of action to get clarity, time to action is almost immediate (sometimes impulsive) and clarity is directly related to the revelations from their actions

2. Shape and reshape ideas, solutions in the process of acting on issues

3. Get others involved and ask for feedback

4. Processes their surroundings as a summary of the overall situation

5. A little information quickly forms a comprehensive but fuzzy perspective of what the situation is, can be, or how it could affect another situation

6. A disorganized but effective, connect as you act process, does poorly with too much structure

7. Reasoning and idea-generating is in non-linear random chunks, testing elements in the action process to connect to the big picture

8. Though they work on multiple projects, usually only can fully concentrate on one situation at a time

9. Resilient; get over negative issues in shorter periods of time compared to others

10. Flexible in unknown environments

11. Makes more mistakes than others but recover faster than others… makes and fixes mistakes in the clarity process of taking action

12. In groups, connecting with others with feedback and random support to requirements as they arise supports success

Liner Processing (Red Brain)

1. Needs Structure to achieve clarity, time to action is dependent on the available structure and the speed at which clarity is achieved

2. Connects tangible elements with logic, organizes information into chunks and cross-references to understand

3. Must have clarity before being comfortable in taking action

4. Identifies and organizes facts and resources before acting

5. less comfortable with unstructured processes or instructions

6. tends to be objective in communication which is often misunderstood as uncaring

7. identifies discrepancies

8. Reasoning and idea-generating uses cross-reference to known references

9. less resilient in situations that are negative or do not show a logical reason for flexibility or change

10. prefers an understanding of a new environment before experiencing them

11. Makes fewer mistakes than others but takes longer to recover from mistakes if a mistake is made, usually start from the beginning by relooking at the facts or resources

12. In groups, specific roles support success

Relational processing (Purple Brain)

1. Needs abundant information to get clarity, time to action is contingent upon the extraction of substantial details relating to the issue

2. All information and experience is related and is

reinforced by the amounts of information for each reference

3.   They take more time to collect and assimilate information compared to others

4.   Prefers clarity before taking action

5.   Connected Information creates options which are compared before for taking action

6.   Less comfortable with little information

7.   Tend to approach organize information into systems and systematic processes

8.   Reasoning and idea-generating is achieved by referencing current and stored information and making comparisons

9.   Related information is internally categorized and connected to other related categories

10.   Less resilient in situations that are negative do not have enough details or options

11.   If they make mistakes, they revisit the original options and information, tend to add a bit more information, then choose the most appropriate option.

12.   While they have a more individual identity, when in groups, they usually want to make sure everyone is aware of the details and are more comfortable with

consistent feedback.

Intuitive Processing (Blue Brain)

1. Achieves clarity through reflection and intuitive referencing of past experiences, time to action is swift but regulated by consistent assimilation of the surroundings and their experience

2. All information and experience is connected on an emotional level (*it must be clarified that there was no specific pattern that showed that subjects were "Emotional"*) in relation to them and their experiences

3. Highly empathetic and sensitive to the environment and people, this information is also included in ambiguity relief processing

4. Take small actions in the process of gathering information and getting a form of sensitivity feedback from the action and it effects

5. More multitasking in thinking process

6. Action or problem-solving is based on personal (intuitive) perspective and may supersede facts and recognized procedures

7. Reasoning and idea-generating is achieved by reflection and referencing the instinctual sensitivity (intuition) from the environment around them

8.   Process efficiency is connected to the people and environment around them

9.   Resilient in most situations, but in circumstances regarding negative emotions, they often take things personally.

10.   Flexible in unknown environments

11.   If they make mistakes, they reflect on their own role in the mistake

12.   In groups, personal understanding of, and connection with the people in the groups support success

As a Green Brain myself, looking through green-colored glasses and interpreting and approaching your world in a green way. I once had a manager, we will call him Steve, who required me to provide details in my reports that I personally felt were only required as his way of torturing me and showing who's boss. I could not see any relevance to actual achievement. I felt I was wasting my time. Time that I could be using to actually do something important instead of adding irrelevant details. I had brought this up a few times, but he insisted the details were important and I was required to find and provide them. I felt he was just out to make my life difficult "how could he really use these effectively" "what actual benefit could they bring, especially with an uncertain outcome where they would likely change anyway" it didn't make sense!

At the time I had no idea of the Colored Brain or Ambiguity Relief, or that he was Purple. All I knew was that he took too much time to make decisions and that he made me waste my time, and neither of these traits elicited my trust or respect. I felt he didn't trust my judgment for my own department, and he felt I was impulsive. I did my job and no longer complained and so we got along, but that did not change the fact that I didn't respect him. While I was respectful, it was only to his face and my emotions remained hidden. Emotions that affected my engagement and limited my motivation to do or be more in the organization.

I eventually found out that he also didn't feel respected by his boss. Apparently, he would spend a substantial amount of time to complete and detailed reports to his boss… who apparently looked only at the summary and didn't look at the rest… and when he had a need for a specific detail, he would ask him rather than look at the report where he had already illustrated it. He felt like he was undervalued.

Now I see this as one of the root causes of why I felt undervalued and even picked on, and why he felt unappreciated and undervalued as well.

If we would have had the awareness of Colored Brain, it would have been easier to accept each other and deal with the emotional issues it created more intelligently.

In a Culture Change initiative we did with Emirates, a senior manager, Jon Francois and one of his top managers, Corina were always arguing, each feeling the others were making their work, and life, difficult.

Jon Francois would usually call Corina to his office and give her a task, in his process of giving the task, he would explain how and create a step by step scenario of how it should be done and what it should look like in the end. Corina however, was ready to go from the moment he had given her the expected result... and would get agitated as he proceeded to explain how he wanted it, especially when she had a better way of doing it... they would argue. When the task was finished, Corina would finish the task, come back to Jon Francois and simply say "It's Done" without an explanation of how it looks... they would argue.

In the program, they were in two different classes where each learned about the colored brain. When Corina found out she was Green, she immediately called Jon Francois and told him, he told her he figured that out and that he was Red... she said she knew... and at the same time, both said: "That's Why!" So, they decided to change their strategy of working with each other.

When Jon Francois would call Corina into his office, he would give her the overall idea then ask if she had any questions. Corina may ask some specifics and then go off and do the task. When it was finished, Corina would come to Jon Francois and give him a clear picture of what she had done and how the end result looked. Their relationship was transformed! Corina felt trusted and performed to her potential. Jon Francois felt respected and was able to focus on leadership rather than management. But, more importantly, the way they dealt with each other, and the energy they created across the whole team was also transformed. The entire team performed better with this new awareness and inspired by the drastic change the saw in Jon Francois and Corina.

Building more trust with Colored Brain

Once an awareness of a non-changeable genetic process of getting clarity is established, you can start with the strategy that Jon Francois and Corina did, work together to create work processes that respect each other's Color.

The next step is to incorporate and use Pre-defined language to connect and show respect while not discounting your own ideas, value, or process. The idea behind Pre-defined communication is that when you have a large set of knowledge related to working with others, an entire concept can be communicated with specific words or phrases that draw a much bigger meaning from that set of knowledge that all people in the conversation are familiar with.

An example of Pre-defined "Colored Brain" language would be: "You are so Green! Remember I am Purple"

This sounds and "feels" much better than: "I need more details and you are not providing them, can you just stop and focus for a moment!"

Because you both have the Colored Brain awareness, what you are saying in essence with Pre-defined communication is: "I understand and accept that you have a genetic Chaotic process of getting clarity which does not lend itself to being very detailed… and I would like to remind you that I have a relational process that requires lots of detail. So, let's find a compromise to work on this together."

Other examples of Colored Brain pre-defined communication may be:

"My Red Brain is working overtime… need to get clear on this first"

"Don't mind me, I'm just doing the Green Brain thing"

"I need to get my Blue team members to help me with this one"

Fear Tolerance and Colored Brain

When you combine the Fear Tolerance with Colored Brain, the intensity of the color changes. It also shows more insights into trust and why it breaks down.

A higher Fear Tolerance increases the element of action in relation to how each brain color gets clarity. However, for a Green Brain, because Greens get clarity through action, this is different than it is for the other colors. A high Fear Tolerance for a Green will simply allow the Green to act more, and take more risk in getting clarity… like saying: "sure, I can do that" when they don't really know-how and try to figure it out as they go. So Greens become darker green.

The Red, Purple and Blue brains, on the other hand, have a lighter color with a higher Fear Tolerance. A Red will need less structure and clarity to make a decision. A Blue will reflect less or require less integration to move forward, and a Purple will need fewer details or less clear options before moving on an idea.

A lower Fear Tolerance has the opposite effect. A Green will take less action and potentially limit the clarity they achieve and so do less. A Red will need more structure and clarity before acting, a Blue will need more reflection and micro-testing, and a Purple will need lots of information and detail.

When we take the kids (Dante and Alessandro) to the beach my wife (a Red Brain) insists they cannot be left alone or go out more than 10 meters from land. Living in Bali where the kids are swimming at least 3 times a week, I (a Green Brain), have full trust in their skill and their judgment, and going out to the bigger waves is fun for both the kids and I. But NOT for my wife! If she feels we have surpassed the barriers of safety, she gets stressed. Besides her high emotional drive for Security, she cannot trust us in a situation that she has no clarity in... And when she knows my lack of attention to detail (and my son Dante's, he is a Green Brain too) is totally unacceptable in a situation where the tides may turn. As a Green Brain though, I am very confident that my and my son's ability to quickly deal with situations as they change, give us the advantage, so it doesn't seem logical to us that she doesn't trust us... This type of different perspectives is where the Colored Brain Gap that kills trust because it just seems so obvious to us!

While my wife does like to swim, she is not fond of swimming in the ocean. The beach is fun for her because it's out of the ordinary place she can relax under an umbrella while getting a massage and watching the kids and I play… but combine a high drive for Security and Control with the need to have or find her Red Brain structure on the ocean beach with two Green Brain's... and you are in for a stretch in maintaining confidence.

For the kids and I, fun is trying to surf, or jumping into big waves as they curl, seeing how far out we can swim and playing rough… although Alessandro, my Red Brained son, while courageous, prefers to not venture out too far. So if we stay within my wife's levels of trust we can all have fun at the beach even if we are not playing together. Because she has the lowest ceiling of trust in the Family, this makes her the "Confidence Influencer" in the team. This means that for the entire family to enjoy an outing, it must be within the levels of confidence of my wife.

Every team has a Confidence Influencer, but not all confidence influencers can be accommodated every time. The acceptance level depends largely on the gap between the individual with the lowest confidence level and the majority… unless of course the person with the lowest confidence happens to be the boss (like my wife). In which case accommodation or at least compromise is essential.

It is important to reiterate that brain color is NOT directly connected to the ability to trust, any of the Ambiguity Relief processes can be totally trusting or not at all. It is the Fear Tolerance combined brain color that determines acceptable guidelines in confidence. Being aware of this creates more trust because you know WHY the dynamic happens. This also helps to not blame those who's levels of confidence, process, or fear tolerance is alien to us… which brings us to the next trust-building strategy.

To learn more about how Colored Brain affects trust, check out my **Colored Brain TEDx talk.**

Making Blame Fun

Blame is the Trust Killer, the biggest villain in our story. It offers no value and kills innovation, proactiveness, and motivation. While some may see blame as a requirement for accountability, there are far better alternatives that are not as damaging to organizational culture.

In the organization where I was head of product development that I had mentioned earlier, my job was exciting in the beginning because it made use of my innovation talent and creative implementation… This drove me to come up with various high potential concepts and ideas to build the organization's profit and profile… but the blaming seeped into the core of my excitement and turned it to frustration.

I often spent extra time working on new ideas that were, in my opinion, more modern and in line with younger and bigger markets. I never felt I was neglecting the older products, but my boss would often blame me for spending time on new stuff… I was also usually blamed if I made a mistake, and in product development, I made a lot of mistakes. The blame brought out my frustration because I knew I could come up with some great products, but the fear of being blamed hindered my self-expression and the desire to innovate. Eventually, I ended up just asking my boss what to do. It was safer, and while I still would get blamed if I didn't execute exactly in line with his idea, following directions was much more palatable and less stressful than being innovative… and so I wasn't. the very reason for my "purpose" and ability to add value had been deleted.

Blame destroys the sense of safety in an environment. It creates risk in innovation or proactive action. It distracts people from focusing on the solution and focuses on justification or recovery of our Emotional Drive of Recognition. It creates chemical reactions in our brains that hinder intelligent action. We become reactive looking for ways to instantly maintain our sense of value… but overall, trust is eroded with every blaming and we compensate to avoid adapting and usually using less of our potential.

But this was not only my problem; it was a big problem in many organizations. In fact, in some organizations, it was a problem that affected Life or Death!

Long ago in the Singapore Government hospital group, Singhealth (as well as many hospitals throughout the globe), if a nurse or doctor would make a mistake in the type of medication or dosage of the medication, there were big consequences to answer to. You could be severely reprimanded (blamed), fired, or even worse through the lawyers!

Needless to say, it was much safer to keep quiet if you made this type of mistake… so reporting was minimal. This did not mean there wasn't a problem, only that the problem wasn't reported.

To deal with the issue in our culture change initiatives or consulting, we usually implement a NO BLAME ZONE. In this case, we hadn't gamified it yet... but here is what happened.

So while some of the management of Singhealth was reluctant, they agreed to have a Blame free policy. But this would be put to the test sooner than they expected.

It was almost 2am in KK hospital (one of the 5 institutions governed by Singhealth). A nurse had administered medication to a patient, shortly after the patient went into cardiac arrest. She realized that she had given the wrong dosage of the medication.

Immediately she reported it. Because of this, the Doctors in the ER knew exactly what to do and the patient's life was saved.

But, it didn't end here. Due to the severity of the situation, the patient's Doctor and the hospital Director were called to the hospital to assess and investigate the situation. It was 3am!

Almost immediately, the Doctor started to blame the nurse, who was already in tears due to her mistake. The Director immediately stopped the Doctor and referenced the no blame policy and the fact that reporting the issue saved the patient's life. They identified the reasons for the mistake and the nurse was commended for identifying and reporting her mistake so promptly.

The story of the incident spread throughout the entire group. Over the next months, reporting shot up drastically, each incident investigated without blame.

Now armed with the data from the various unintentional mistakes, the administration was able to identify the root causes of the problems and fix them. Communication processes and policies were modified, training was implemented… Shortly the actual problem was drastically reduced.

NO BLAME saved lives!

In a more recent initiative, the No Blame zone has been lightly gamified to change the meaning of blame and make it fun…

Yes, blame can be fun!

The first step in creating a no-blame zone is to get the sign. We have prepared a cool one for you at: www.NoBlame.zone

Download it then print out lots of copies in color. Then explain to your team why you want to create a no-blame zone. Get their buy into the idea of being blame-free. Resistance will appear from chronic blamers! …and they will want to know how people can be held accountable without blame… and yes, there is an alternative to blame we will share shortly.

But first, the eradication of blame.

I should mention that keeping a positive spin on "No Blame" like "respect others", or "be patient"… do NOT have the same effect… You MUST use the "B" word to make it fun and work. Why? Because of contrast and sarcasm… the brother and sister of humor. Changing the meaning of something serious and stressful by using it in a light and carefree way.

For example:

Choose Jane… "Today, anything that goes wrong Jane's fault!" Obviously, Jane is not responsible for everything. This makes no sense… and that is the point. This is called contrast.

Now let's say Jane is about to start a new project and she is worried about the outcome… "Don't worry Jane, if it doesn't work, we will just Blame you!"

Bringing the "B" word out in the open makes it easier to be aware of blame. Considering most people don't wake up in the morning and think… "today, my target is to blame 5 people ", blame is not an intention, it is a reaction. The more awareness we have, the easier it is to take control. But it's not always easy to catch yourself before you blame and so to really create awareness at the right time, we need to catch people blaming! But we cannot blame them for blaming and they are probably not in the best of emotional state when they are so we need a positive awareness strategy.

Try this:

Smile! I mean really smile… like now! Now say while you are smiling "Are you blaming?"

Did you chuck a little? You would have if you were really smiling because it's contrasting the norm.

After you have Downloaded the sign and explained the concept to everyone, here are the steps to a successful and fun NO BLAME ZONE:

- Share how they can keep blame in the open and fun

- Share the "Are you blaming" strategy and get them to try it on the spot

- Get them to acknowledge to each other that they will accept no blame feedback and support each other not to blame

- Explain the alternative to blame and get agreement

So what is the alternative to blame? Failing Intelligently

There are 3 steps to failing intelligently

1. **Make sure the person is aware of the consequences.**

I was contracted to do a series of programs for Etisalat, a UAE telco provider who required me to do two 3-hour keynotes, one in the morning and one in the afternoon, at each of their 7 offices. The first was in Dubai at an auditorium that seated 210 people. It was a Sunday, the first day of the workweek in the UAE. The HR director and the HR manager were there to ensure a smooth program. By the time everyone came in, the entire audience consisted of 21 people!

After the first talk, the HR director was furious with the HR manager. She blamed her for the low attendance and told her she had better fill the room for the afternoon session... then she left!

I was left alone with the HR manager who proceeded to complain to me about how unfair her boss was. I felt that this focus would not serve the desired outcome, so I asked her some questions.

"How are you going to get a full house?" I asked. "It's not possible! I sent out emails and SMS before the weekend, they must be responsible to make their own time to attend. I do not control other people's schedules!" she replied...

To illustrate the consequences, I told her that I believed her boss was looking at it from a value perspective for the company. I explained that based on how much I was being paid for the 3-hour talk, divided by the 21 people who showed up created a very expensive per person cost. I suggested that her boss might feel her investment was not being optimized. And just helping her to do the math, gave her the perspective that she could understand why her boss was angry.

2. Make sure they solve the problem immediately

"What will you do?" I asked. "The same as I did last time. Send emails and SMS to their phones." "Will that work?" I replied.

"No! Soon everyone will go out for lunch and when they come back they won't likely read their email in time. And since Etisalat provides free phone service to employees, most men give the SIM card to their wives since they use more airtime… so half will not even see the SMS". She had already been defeated by her own reaction to the situation.

Then I asked the age-old question that is often the source of frustration: "What do you think you could do that actually will work?"

And she uttered the dreaded words: "I don't know!" Unfortunately, this is quite common, but for Failing Intelligently to work, THEY must solve the problem themselves! I think of this problem as the Peanut Butter and Brain Syndrome. Like when peanut butter sticks in your mouth and you need to work it as you eat it. When someone says "I don't know" it's like their brain has peanut butter in it… the gears aren't moving, and you need to work it before you can actually get the answer. So I said, "ok, but if you did know, what would you do?" She squinted her eyes at me and said: "I don't know!"… "I know you don't know, but if you did know, what would you do?" I continued. This went on a few more times with her insisting she did not know what to do… until the peanut butter got worked out, then she had an idea. She said, "actually, I could call the secretaries, they can get to everyone before they go for lunch so they can come directly after." I asked her if she thought that would work, and she said "yes!" …and it did, the second session was packed, people were standing because there were no more seats. She had succeeded, and it was her idea. How do you think she felt? She owned the success and learned in the process, plus gained more confidence. But even if she would have failed, she would have learned, and if there were more events to be had, I could have helped her again to fail intelligently by asking questions that supported her eventual success.

Which leads to the third step.

3. Ask what could be done to prevent the problem in the future.

Now that the peanut butter is unstuck, they will be able to come up with an intelligent plan or strategy. Now they write it down and think it through, refine it and implement it together wherever possible. If it stays in the written stage without any implementation, you lose trust and they may feel their ideas have no value to you, so they stop providing them.

Creating a blame-free environment with the Failing Intelligently alternative will not only improve trust and confidence, it improves competence and innovative problem-solving.

Active Trust

In a no blame environment people will have more confidence to act on what they believe to be the best way to achieve a goal. But this creates another potential issue if you have a high emotional drive of security. This can mess you up when trying to let go and let other people express their value and potential.

This is where "Active Trust" needs to be part of the game. Active Trust means exactly that, you actively trust someone... even if you don't trust them! Confused? Because of the different genetic Ambiguity Relief processes, there will always be situations where you know your way is better than others, and there will be times after you have expressed your way of doing things, that others still want to do it their own way. And you cannot see how this will work... but if you don't let them try, they will never know and while they may not tell you, they blame you internally for not giving them a chance. Plus, they know you don't trust them and this counteracts the whole build an environment of trust thing. So, Active Trust means that you give them a chance, even if you think they will fail.

From here 2 things happen:

1. They surprise you and succeed and respect you for letting them show their worth.

2. They fail and they respect you for letting them try.

But now they also have a sense of reciprocity because you trusted them and they let you down, so they try to make it up to you more because… you trusted them.

Trust will be the foundation the organizational culture gameboard will sit on. Without it, building a high performing culture with people who live up to their potential will be difficult. Apply these strategies and you will see a drastic and very visible result in how people connect with each other and perform:

- **Repositioning Fear Tolerance -** when one person has a high Fear Tolerance, and another has a low one, perceptions of the right amount of risk or even what is a risk and what is not, create scenarios where the actions surrounding the perception kill trust.

- **Colored Brain -** when others do not understand us due to our genetic clarity processing differences or try to push a process on us that we feel is not supporting our success, fear is ignited because we feel our ability to add values is reduced.

- **Pre-defined Communication** - incorporate and use Pre-defined language to connect and show respect while not discounting your own ideas, value, or process.

- **Identify Confidence Influencers** - the acceptance level of ideas or plans depend largely on the gap between the individual with the lowest confidence level and the majority.

- **Making Blame Fun** – creating a No Blame Zone and apply the Failing Intelligently strategy

- **Active Trust** - actively trust someone… even if you don't trust them

The Secret Amulet of "Measure Everything"

Delving deeper into the game mechanics, we find the Amulet of MeasureEverything. The single most important element to productive gamification! Measurement is the means by which we decide, feel, validate, and act on anything. It can inspire positive or negative emotions and motivation.

Types of measurement we constantly use are:

- Comparison

- Quantity

- Quality

- Time

- Frequency

- Milestones

- Objective

- Value

Gamification of measurement is also regularly used in everyday life, although we may not notice it. We use it in

- LEVELS

  o PhD

  o Superstar

  o Manager

- QUALITY

  - ○ Gold standard

  - ○ Accredited

  - ○ 98% Pure

- COMPARISON

  - o Improved

  - o 1st place

- TIME

  - o 30-day challenge

  - o 15-minute delivery

- QUANTITY

  - o 23 likes

  - o Viewed 88 times

- OBJECTIVE

  - o 28" waist

  - o 0 defects

While these labels are not necessarily meant for gamification, the gamified emotional value to the labels is very real.

Measurement is happening all around us, when we compare ourselves with others when setting goals, and even assess the quality of our relationships. Measurement is part of our need to validate ourselves and our lives. As an author, How Many people read my book (at least the first chapter) matters to me. The fact that you are reading this is a validation of my ideas and thoughts. Even if you do not agree with or like my concepts, I have a sense of purpose that is identified with at least providing insight for you to ponder.

Others may measure how many people who read their book LIKE and share their ideas. This now limits the sense of validation and it becomes more difficult to get the positive emotions associated with it. Others may measure their ability to make the New York Times Bestseller list, and while that would be Super Cool, it massively limits the ability to feel you are achieving a purpose.

We also need to consider how long it takes before we can measure. If my measurement rule required me to finish a book before I felt my emotional drive for Achievement fulfilled... I probably would not have finished this book. But because I can manage my sense of validation by measuring simple things, small progress and milestones like reading some of my passages with my kids or being grateful for new inspiration, I am constantly feeling a strong sense of validation as a human being, meaning I truly feel my life has purpose.

So, measuring things that are difficult or take a long time to achieve do not support our daily emotional gratifications and our personal sense of value... which brings us to the Amulet of MeasureEverything.

When measurement rules in the workplace change, so do the

culture and the engagement… and confidence and competence.

Most organizations measure KPIs. While that's all good, THERE IS NOTHING IN BETWEEN! And it can take a long time to meet your KPIs… and what if you don't meet them… and how do you know you are on the right track? This leaves us with gaps and lack of clarity and therefore potential lack of consistent validation and emotional gratification leaving us, disengaged and on the road of underachievement.

What if we worked this backward?

Last year my sons, Dante and Alessandro who were 10 and 7 at the time, wrote books in 2 months. If you have kids, you will understand it is often a chore just to get them to do homework let alone write a book. To achieve this, we needed to provide a constant source of emotional gratification to the entire book project which not only included writing the book, but designing the cover, illustrating the images and digitizing them, getting sponsors, dealing with the printers, and putting it up on Amazon KDP.

We did make the milestones and celebrated at each one, but we went one step further in the spirit of MeasureEverything, we identified the behaviors that would help them succeed and we measured and rewarded (emotionally) these behaviors daily. We also measured attitude, above-average quality, teamwork, and creative ideas.

The result: "The History of Life – 50 Fun Facts to Make You Sound Very Smart" a 72-page book by Dante Carmazzi. And

"The Adventures of Slappy the Crocodile" a 28-page storybook by Alessandro Carmazzi. The books are available on Amazon and they even made a website, www.DnAbooks.net to promote them.

If we measure only results, the behaviors and emotions to help us achieve those results are assumed but may not be nurtured enough to support the achievement. But if we measure everything leading up to the result, the journey is easier, we have more clarity and emotional validation to more confidently actualize the result.

Imagine you have a goal. You are doing your best to achieve the goal and deal with distractions and other work that comes your way. You may even have a deadline for the goal. But when you finally achieve the goal, you think back to better ways you would have achieved it or identified mistakes that delayed the goal. What if you already had an idea based on past experience of what behaviors, attitudes, and collaborations would support the achievement of the goal. Even if we already know, we do get distracted and often side-tracked. If these behaviors and attitudes were measured consistently, we would constantly be reminded of our success formula… and adhere to it more effectively, usually creating better, faster results!

The quality and strategy of measurement are important too. Quality measurement is fast and instant measurement, providing feedback at the moment a behavior is exhibited, when the behavior is clear and in perspective. To have clarity in the first place, you should have a clear idea of what the behavior looks like, sounds like, and feels like. This strategy is where things get tricky.

Confession of a car salesman

I used to work as a car salesman in the summer when I was going to university. When I was new, I was very excited about selling lots of cars and making lots of money, I soon found out these two were not mutually exclusive. The dealership had 2 "leaderboards". One with the number of cars that were sold and the salesman who sold them... and another with the salesmen who made the most commissions. I quickly rose to the #2 spot of who sold the most cars but was usually 2nd to last on the profit board. How did that work? I was always trying to give the best deal to my clients, I was genuine and caring so clients felt comfortable with me and they would buy... unfortunately, giving them the best deal left little commission for me. While the #1 sales guy, Max, who was also the #1 profit guy was able to make people feel great about paying more. Because I was always in the top sales list I continued to work hard to stay there, the top commissions' list, on the other hand, I would justify that my values were more important than the money... but I really did want the money. Yet wanting the money was not enough, the fact was that I liked being liked more than I liked the money. It was my Emotional drive of Love & Belonging that was higher than the emotions attached to what the money would bring me.

The measurement maintained the motivation to stay on top for sales, but to be a high producer the motivators were not defined to match my primary emotional drivers. It was not until I had an incident that things changed. A pretty young lady named Tammy came to see me looking for a car and I found the perfect one for her. She had brought 2 of her large male friends with her to make sure she did not get ripped off. Fortunately, I told her, you got me, I will take care of you. I sincerely meant that, but she and her friends were naturally skeptical. I had set her up to literally get the best deal and gave her instructions on what to do when the closer came to talk to her. Max was the closer, and he came in and did his thing with amazing finesse, and she was taken by him to the point she ignored my instructions, when he left, I reinstructed her what to do, at this time she freaked out, lost all trust and left. The next day the dealership sold the car to another dealership for the amount I was trying to sell Tammy the car. A week later, Tammi walks back in looking for the car telling me she saw an identical one at another dealership for a thousand dollars more. I told her that it was the same car. She was sad.

The day before Tammi had come in, Max had sold an SUV 4x4 to a newly married couple, he made a $6000 commission on it and the couple was ecstatic for the deal they got. They were so grateful, they even brought him cookies the following day. I now compared the emotional gratification for the Love & Belonging I valued with the situation from Tammy and his success with the couple… There was a very big gap. I realized that I did not need to give away profit to achieve a customer's high level of satisfaction. I realized my behavior was incongruent with the emotions I was trying to achieve. I realized that money was not a factor for customer satisfaction. This led to a quest to identify his behaviors and emulate them.

After understanding his skill and behaviors, and adapting it to my own style, I did go up on the second list but not that much. While I never beat him, I did learn many lessons and, at least for the rest of the summer, made more money.

The measurement only measured results, never behaviors. I had never even been taught the behaviors or had any alignment from sales to my primary emotional drives, and so it took a while for me to figure this out. But imagine if you knew what behaviors would not only achieve the objectives but also fulfill more emotional drives.

I realized that my position on the top sales list was my primary motivation, I tried harder and put more effort into learning the best way to stay on that list. But also found myself minimizing the value of the top profit list to compensate for and justify my position on the top sales list. I would think to myself, if I make too much profit, they may not send their friends and I won't make more sales… The motivation was to stay on the list I had already made, even at the expense of the full profit potential that I had realized was possible. This motivation came from seeing my progress on the top sales list and not wanting to let it go.

The other sales guys became less motivated.

I also noticed that the other sales guys who were usually at the bottom of the list, usually stayed at the bottom of the list. Many of these people had been there longer than I had and had more skill, yet their motivation and ultimately their results weren't there.

Since the lower level, sales guys were usually always the lower level sales guys, and the top sales guys were usually always the top sales guys, the top 4 and the bottom 4 were usually the established groups. Each group would usually stay in their corner unless there was some uncommon disruption. Just like me, the people who made the top group would fight to stay there, while the bottom group became complacent with their position since it seemed like no matter what they tried they would seldom make it to the top group. The reality was, they did not fight as hard to move forward as the top guys fought to make sure they did not go backward.

To achieve more "Success Motivation" (motivation fuelled by an existing success), people need to see they are making progress in something. And because we don't always take the initial initiative, a work gamification system needs to push people to get there, and this is where measurement stagey comes in...

Measuring to initiate success

When you feel like you are succeeding and making progress (the emotional drive for achievement), you gain momentum. This "progress" is a power we can harness by creating scenarios that initiate success motivation...

My car sales experience taught me that for most people, not going backward in status or achievement is a much stronger motivator than achieving something new. Once you have achieved something, losing it, or the potential to lose it, motivates you to take actions that will prevent loss.

In a work gamification system, this means that once you have attained a certain level, status on a list or group, or achieved certain recognition, you will be motivated to keep it... and potentially even do more to get to the next level. So if we find ways to create a level of success for more than the aggressive few, we can increase performance across the board.

Both my sons Dante and Alessandro play chess. Alessandro has generally been a better player and usually beats Dante. After a while, Dante didn't really like to play with him as much since his younger brother was beating him. So we made some new rules. Each player would not take advantage of silly moves or unseen danger and would support the other to not make a silly move. The purpose was to focus on strategy and not on a lack of focus. But there was a hidden agenda, Dante's biggest downfall was his lack of focus that made him lose lots of pieces that he did not know were in danger. I know that if he had an opportunity to win, his interest would be reignited, and his skill would follow.

The result was that Dante would win more often. Suddenly, his interest peaked, and he was much more excited to play. Of course, Alessandro was now even more interested to improve since he was winning less than he used to.

The result: both kids improved their motivation and their chess skill... even their focus to spot danger in the game improved.

As shown in chapter Technology vs. Humanity, anticipation is the primary "feel good" motivation. If we feel we cannot achieve something with the effort we are able to exert, or we feel that our skillset is not enough to make something happen… we give up and focus on what we are good at, which may be watching TV and being able to recite past episodes of "Friends" from memory… probably not the most useful skill.

To succeed and improve, we must continue to stretch our potential. To lead others to success we must be able to navigate enough success and enough fun to keep people anticipating that potential and all the benefits that come from additional competency.

How can measuring behaviors create more Success Motivation without creating complacency groups?

Each type of measurement can be used in measuring behavior and there will usually be different behaviors that will support specific types of results. Highlighting measurement results of the multiple success related behaviors in a game structure will ultimately build a Success Motivation gamified strategy when theming. The creation of relevant structures to support a **Challenging** enough behavior modification can create more **Anticipation** of achieving personal **Potential** through **Comparison**… which will ultimately lead to Personal **Validation** and the need to evolve from there to the next level creating continuous improvement.

BONUS: Finding the emotional drives that motivate those behaviors and including them in the game structure will make the behavior modification MORE exciting and easier to meet any potential challenges faced.

Reaching the Higher Levels
of Performance

Chapter introduction by Rhiannon Rees

#1 Business and Performance Coach (IAOTP) -2019 and #6 Global Guru - Coaching

I have spent decades in the field of human performance and potential (behavior).

Working with a variety of clients including Celebrities, Elite Athletes, Olympians, and Entrepreneurs as well as anyone else who knows that a better life exists on the other side of their comfort zone.

Arthur's work in Organizational Culture is peppered with absolute moments of sheer brilliance gained from his profession and life which are reflected in a concise and practical way in this essential handbook for every organization.

The key points most notable are: Each individual is uniquely gifted with talent and skillsets that no one else has. The magic happens when these gifts are not only "discovered" - they are actually harnessed in any situation.

How you play the game - is ultimately how you play the game of life.

Arthur's brilliant tip around the Squali app - means that this can be put into a practical perspective. I mean who doesn't have 20 seconds to measure performance in any given situation?

This is further expanded on in my book "Life is a Choice and the Choice is Yours" (www.consciouscoaching.coach), which also introduces a handful of experts in their field - again maximizing human potential. Not only will you find many parallels, suggesting truth to this research but new applications to your own personal development.

Arthur's work will make a massive difference to your team and your business.

I encourage you to take this book with you and create a lasting legacy in whatever field or faculty you are in..

The question people often ask is: "Are there recipes for high performance?" The answer is always yes and no. Certain structures of motivated competence (competence that people act on passionately) appear over and over again for specific types of group mixes and individual behaviors... but, even though people may have the same competencies, and the same emotions and motivations that drive implementation of those competencies, how each person experiences the motivation is unique.

But if we know the fundamental motivator, we can support the behavior that will lead to high performance, which means... We can predict the performance and design high performing teams. And, if we can create game elements to support it and the desired behavior, we can nurture cultures and individuals who apply newly motivated competence.

Enter the Game Elements

When we look at the world of games, there are recurring structures and elements that make people want to play or watch it.

The measures of performance do not always require someone to lose, but they are required to have winners. Work gamification in relation to organizational culture must cultivate winners to maintain passion... but a winner who always wins becomes complacent, and they must be "challenge" in order to maintain and even grow higher levels of performance. So while we don't want people to "Lose" we do not want them to always win!

If there are no losers, how do we win? Measurement creates opportunities to set benchmarks. We can measure against our own performance, a standard of performance, or even an industry competitor.

In the early days of privatized telecommunication in the US (yes, I am that old), AT&T was the industry leader. A new player came to market, MCI with one objective... "Beat AT & T " they had various measurements on which to beat the industry giant and were rewarding people and teams who supported the initiative and produced results. they had created multiple opportunities to WIN! Geography, number of long-distance calls, revenue, PR... were only a few of the elements used to measure a win. Of course, in today's PFB era, the timeline has moved drastically and our time to measurement needs to have almost instant feedback to maintain the levels of motivation.

As a completely new player in the industry, MCI eventually became the second biggest next to AT&T. And they did it with only the single focus of "beat AT&T". The benchmark was AT&T's numbers, and the motivation was the emotions of anticipation of hitting and beating those numbers. The closer they got to the benchmark, the harder the people worked, and once they met one benchmark goal, they were more excited about the next and the anticipation was easier to feel... perpetuating motivation and making the numbers.

The staff of MCI never lost, but they did not always win. Some months AT&T would do holiday campaigns and MCI would lose some of the wins that had previously... but the people never FELT lost within MCI they were on a quest and they had a constant sense of anticipation for the next win... AT&T had been a monopoly and was depicted as a heartless conglomerate that would callously disconnect grandma's phone service if she was late paying her long-distance phone bill. This was a quest and it was portrayed as the little guy united against the uncaring giant that had little compassion for the average person or small business. They felt they were the good guys fighting the big bad villain. Any losses in traction for beating AT&T were simply setbacks to the inevitable win... good shall always triumph over evil. The theme was set and it supported a sense of purpose beyond the job.

It sounds confusing! People should win and not lose, but not always win...?!? Themes...?

Most team sports have multiple levels of "Win State". Football (Soccer for our North American readers) has multiple professional leagues, and ultimately prestigious the World Cup. Teams have various benchmark measures, but players also have their ranks and play across the professional and the country representation World Cup matches.

The World Cup starts with a qualification at the level of geography: City, State, Region, and finally Country, but only 15 people are chosen to represent the country. And only 32 teams will play. Some never even have a chance to play.

It begins with individual competencies at a local city level. Players who show competencies are promoted to state and if individual competence continues within a team environment, they may eventually be promoted to represent the county. Meanwhile, these teams still compete against each other creating opportunities to show individual and team potential.

But each geography supports a win state. Even qualifying to be on the local team is a win for the individual and being a part of the country team is just a much bigger win. But the anticipation and potential are always there to be promoted to the next level. The motivation to reach the next level has the potential to breed more competency, discipline, and dedication.

If the individual reaches the country stage, the individual becomes less important than the team and the teams must now qualify to be allowed to even participate in the World Cup Game.

The different county teams compete, countries are ranked, and eventually, one team wins the World Cup. But the fact that the teams that play even got to play are enough of a win to create more anticipation for the various other elements of personal and team competency.

This is a game mechanism.

A series of structures creating multiple opportunities to win and develop which are measured through both team and personal competency.

So if we apply the idea to behavior and competency which are connected to larger organizational outcomes, we create easier, more frequent wins that become more stringently measured as one produces both team and individual results.

If we relate the World Cup example to an organization: City-level would measure only the behaviors needed to achieve the required results, but it also includes the behavior of the overall team. State promotes those with a consistent behavior to teams that show more promise and potential for achievement. Region now looks at individual and team results and compares elements such as Engagement to other organizations. In addition to the behavior, how they may support others to also achieve the desired behaviors and higher performance (leadership). At the county level, these people are regularly exhibiting the behaviors and have a track record of results in line organizational objectives. But more importantly, this group also wins when they support others to get promoted to be on the team. The competition here need not be each other, but specific benchmarks related to organizational culture or engagement, they may be related to innovation and be measured on a monthly basis. While the behaviors are still being measured across the board daily to keep people on track.

Daily!!!! Impossible!!!

Enter Squadli, the Performance measurement gamification app/dashboard.

The biggest barrier to effective performance measurement is time. Most performance measurement is done biannually or annually… and it takes lots of time to "review". Unfortunately, most of the review is usually from the previous 3 to 4 weeks because that is what we remember more clearly. It is also the time when people perk up and start to be more efficient.

But when we are measuring behaviors, acknowledging a behavior only takes a few seconds. With the Squali app, the entire record of who, what, how and why are logged and graphed in less than 20 seconds. This allows daily observation and recording of the behaviors with the same amount of time it takes to write a WhatsApp message. Here is how it works:

Setup

1.	Set a team name (you can have multiple teams)

2.	Invite your team members

3.	Determine the number of team members for your TOP LIST (Ex. If you have 50 members in your team, your top list may be the top 10)

4.	Set the behavior objectives (I personally recommend no more than eight)

5.	Set the awards and their point values (I personally use the ones that come with the app)

6.   Set top-down, 360, or 360 + peer to peer (I personally use the full peer to peer 360 setting)

Use in 20 seconds or less

1.   Observe a behavior

2.   Choose team member who exhibited the behavior from the team menu

3.   Choose an emoji related to how you feel about the behavior (there are positive and negative emotions with +/- points) or an award (I give more points to the awards and make them more special)

4.   Choose the behavior objective it connects to

5.   Identify the specifics in less than 200 characters

6.   Choose if it should be:

   a. private (only you see it)

   b. visible (you and the team member can see it)

   c. public (the whole team can see it)

7.   Push send

If you have chosen the 360 peer to peer, you will have four filters to observe the results:

–   Your own as a team leader

–   The feedback they give each other

–   The combined feedback

- The feedback the team sends you

Based on the points each gets; they will be ranked on a list. If you have chosen your Top List to have 10, only the team members within the top 10 point scores are ranked, everyone else's rank says: "You are not in the top 10" but based on what we discussed, it would be likely that the same people usually achieve the top 10 and that would demotivate the rest! And this is why I like this app so much because each behavior objective has its own list… which gives an opportunity for everyone else to also be on at least one or more lists. I may not be on the main list, but if I am on the "Innovation" list, I feel acknowledged and have the anticipation of possibly getting to the top 10… after all, I could be #11 and just need to work a little harder on some of the rest of the behaviors to get there.

While there are many more strategies and features to use the simplicity of the Squadli app and the web dashboard… it is best you discover it further on www.squadli.com. It is important to note that Squadli is a tool to support work gamification… it is not as the full solution. The key benefits of this tool are:

- You can define and measure behaviors daily

- You can have multiple focused teams to make it easy to create "Game Clusters". These teams can also compete against each other or benchmarks to reinforce team performance and cross team/department cooperative behaviors

- You can give fast easy feedback

- You can achieve game-state with ranking

- You can create more anticipation across team members with multiple lists for each of the Behavior Objectives

- You can give negative feedback in positive ways to improve performance and give clarity

- You can use the concept of scarcity to build more value to being on the list to keep sustainability.

Using Squadli with a combined team and individual strategy allows the creation of an easy to understand level ascension game strategy. This strategy provides the anticipation of moving up as an individual as well as part of the team and gaining emotional drives of:

- Achievement

- Recognition

- Love & Belonging

- Security

- Diversity

- Challenge & Growth

So basically most of the emotional drives! …which means… if it is led properly, and it has a compelling game structure, gamifying performance measurement can make work addictively fun!

This brings us to the next level of successful work gamification:

Leadership – or, becoming the Game Master!

The Digital Transformation Pre-Formation

The big thing is Digital Transformation. And most people are aware that it requires organizational Culture change... but most organizations start before they are ready, and while the rewards are big, the cost in time and money to initiate it is vast and, according to a McKenzie Digital "Unlocking success in digital transformations" study, most of the initiatives they surveyed had success rates between 4% and 11% and up to 26% in the Tech industry... and those numbers SUCK!

Another study by the Economist Intelligence Unit, on the other hand, shows that those who have succeeded are showing profitable results in as little as 2 years and 72% of say Organizational Culture Change is required for the success of a Digital Transformation initiative. So if you get it going IT WILL PAY OFF!

But WHY do most organizations fail in Digital Transformation efforts?

If they do culture change, organizations often start their culture change initiatives at the same time they begin their Digital Transformation initiatives... and most of the time, the culture is Not Ready! Too much to do without an "evolved" organizational culture and the whole thing falls through. And, if their culture change initiatives are top-down... they are almost certainly Doomed to ultimate Failure!

But the solution is not complicated or expensive when we apply elements of measurement and gamification. It all starts with benchmarking how evolved your organizational culture is to get an idea if it's aggressive and agile enough to make it through the Disruption Responsiveness hump.

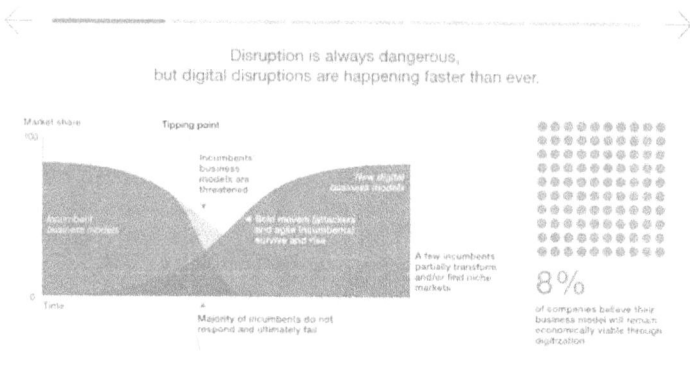

Think of a game, disruption is often part of the challenge or obstacle, and yet we have fun overcoming the chaos to achieve a win. A gamified work process affects how evolved a culture is, and the level of culture evolution affects its agility and level of commitment, which is required to overcome disruption.

There are 5 Levels of Culture Evolution. You can see more detail online in the *"Ultimate Guide to Leading Organizational Change"*:

The Blame Culture – little trust, people wait to be told what to do, and little cooperation or innovation.

The Multi-Directional Culture – people are cliquish within their departments, but low trust and cooperation with management or other departments.

The Live and Let Live Culture – things get done but people are complacent and lack passion and creativity.

The Brand Congruent Culture – people believe in the product or service and support each other to expand on it. Innovation and passion are supported through processes, management, and culture.

The Leadership Enriched Culture – leadership is the role of everyone, and most are firm believers in the brand and the organization. Being creative about building the business supports excitement and people feel a sense of ownership.

Digital Transformation requires a culture that is agile and has an established sense of trust. To succeed in a Digital Transformation initiative, the minimum requirement of culture evolution would be the Brand Congruent Culture.

The reason most organizations attempting Digital Transformation fail is that they are only evolved to the Live and Let Live culture at best. And that is being generous! Based on the DCI culture evolution study that began in 2017, 61% of organizations are still in the Blame Culture. Only 9% of organizations make it to the Brand Congruent Culture and 4% to the Leadership Enriched culture.

Which seems to correlate with McKenzie's success rates.

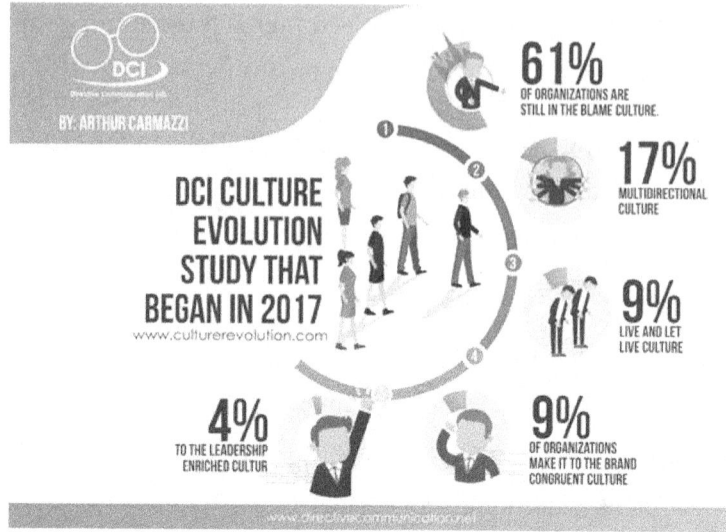

To evolve to a Brand Congruent culture, you need to develop the right psychology, and there are 3 psychological factors created through work gamification that support an evolved culture that will be sustainable and agile.

1.   A stakeholder (employee) created a set of guiding principles (behaviors) to ensure a great culture for all to succeed in. [Measured through Squadli]

2.   A systematic way to support people to express and personally feel their value to the organization and its objectives while applying their desired set of behaviors. [Game rewards and levels]

3.   A measurement system to measure the and visibly communicate the No. 1 and No. 2 [Game feedback and measurement connected to Win State]

So here are the 5 steps to take BEFORE Digital Transformation

1. Benchmark your current organizational culture evolution! This is done with the OCEAN Culture Evolution Assessment at *www.cultureevolution.com*. You will need perspectives from a minimum of 20% of the organization at different levels (Senior Management, Middle Management, and non-management) to get a usable understanding.

2. Identify the gaps from where you are to where you need to be and gamify the evolution process.

3. Share your results and culture goals with everyone. Include the description of what the Goal Culture will be like. Gamify the visualization of progress.

4. Begin your initiative with the above 3 factors in mind. Get the "Key Influencers" and everyone involved in feedback and implementation for making it happen. Also include Colored Brain and Emotional Drive Elements to support communication, trust, and motivation. There are 3 elements that are essential for success in this step:

   a. It must be a top guided, Bottom-Up initiative (more detail online in the *"Ultimate Guide to Leading Organizational Change"*)

   b. Desired behaviors must be measured often to show progress (Use Squadli)

   c. The people of the organization must see fast results to maintain momentum (Gamified visual feedback)

5. After 4 to 6 weeks, test the culture again to see progress and compare the graphs and evolution improvement. Share the progress and how ready (or close to ready you are). Sharing the measured progress supports motivation and excitement that the people are achieving the results they have set out to achieve. Showing progress, Team and Individual contribution, and visible progress through gamified feedback systems create an even bigger impact.

To succeed in a specific in a Pre-Digital Transformation Culture Change Initiative, the behaviors should be related to:

− Innovation

− Agility

− Proactive actions

− Fast decisions

− Active trust (trusting people even if you don't really trust them)

− Synergizing/Leveraging with people who have different Ambiguity Relief Processes (Genetic process of getting clarity)

− Short impactful meetings

− Open communication (Identify and relate Communication process: *www.coloredbrain.com*)

- No Blame (see *www.noblame.zone*)

Every change initiative has resistance... but remember, people, do not resist change. Imagine someone shows up at your door and hands you $10 Million to change your life... chances are you will not say, "Na, I'm good!" ...you will most likely embrace the change and take the money.

What people resist in "Stupid Stuff", something they feel will not benefit them or just makes life more difficult. But when the people are creating the culture in a top guided bottom-up initiative, they own it, they are creating the change they want. And it is not about getting more salary (this should be predefined just in case), it is about creating a Clear, Supportive, Trusting, and Fun working environment where they can "feel" personally successful in the process of achieving organizational objectives?

Once the people are on board and excited about the possibilities and feel they can visibly help the organization and its brand with their own creativity... and you have a gamified feedback system to regularly show personal, team, and organizational progress... you are set to begin the Digital transformation efforts.

Culture Evolution through Gamification has just increased your chances of Digital Transformation success by 300%

Choosing the Leader Avatar, Do you Measure up?

Anytime you begin a new initiative, people need to adopt it, and leadership will be the key to making fun at work, work.

While everyone wants to have fun, remember that a personal sense of value is still more important. Some may perceive that having fun is counter to adding value and reject potential rewards and the fun that goes with it.

…and forcing people to "Have Fun" and be a part of a gamified work process will not have the effect we are looking for.

There are 4 factors to establishing the bases for leading a work gamification initiative:

1. The gamified process must be created by the people who do the work

    a. While this may sound like common sense, often we find management deciding that their skill in creating the game is better than the people who do the work… without an in-depth understanding of the work itself and the pains, struggles, and excitement people have through the work, it is difficult to create a systematic and motivating game process relative to goal attainment in that specific work.

    b. As a leader, you would need to recruit the individuals who are in the job and guide them to build a gamified work process through the 8 steps of gamification (in the next chapter)

2. Implementation requires action

    a. Even though it may be fun and people who innovate and create the gamified work may be excited about it… they still get busy and may not initiate its implementation, sometimes because they are not fully secure in the belief that the leader is "Really" behind it.

    b. As a leader, you must work with the team who innovated the game to make sure it starts and fine-tune it as you go

3. Be part of the fun

    a. This cannot be about "the staff", management also needs to be a part of the game and held by the same rules and behaviors as others

4. Be visible

    a. Make sure the communications department is set to share and promote the feedback, results, and highlights of the game AND that these are shared referencing increases in productivity, engagement, communication, cooperation, culture evolution… or whatever you are aiming for

    b. As a leader, create your own communications on how you feel about the progress everyone is making

But what if you are no fun? What if there is a barrier because you are in a management position? What if people just perceive you as only Serious? What if people just don't trust you?

I once made the mistake that because I was the head of the department, that people will listen to me and do what I say. Assuming of course that they would willingly and happily do it out of a sense of responsibility for their job. ZERRR!

In my inexperience I managed to alienate a key player, let's call her Cindy, in the department, turn an intermediary, let's call her Jane, into a backstabbing advisory, and found justifications to blame it all on them.

After realizing what I had done, I tried to reverse the problem with Cindy, I apologized, tried doing favors… anything I could… but it was too late. Eventually, Cindy, a lady that had been there 13 years before I came, quit and no one else was adept to take up her slack… and of course, management blamed me for her quitting.

I tried to fix things with Jane by giving her credit, supporting her ideas… but that was too late too! She was out to prove my inadequacy as a leader and manager. While she was right, I was good enough at politics to manage to get her to quit. All this focus and defensiveness prevented me and both of these ladies from focusing on the real work… we were too busy trying to make each other wrong and ourselves look good while the organization was getting NOTHING from our negative energy. And none of us had any type of fulfillment in the process… just more stress.

We don't go into a job to suck as a leader or to be good at politics. While we get work to have a sense of security in our lives, we join to do a good job and make a real impact. It is how we act and react to the environment that affects what we think will support us in doing that or not, and the more we need to defend against bad management or red tape or antiquated policy... the less we are able to really focus on the organizational objectives.

So our job as a leader in gamifying work to create astounding organizational cultures is largely in finding the factors that show how this will benefit the majority. These may include:

- Showing that the "Game" will help them achieve the Ideal Work Environment

   o This "Ideal Work Environment" is part of a study we did across 57 countries with everyone from CEOs to Janitors, PhDs to Highschool dropouts, multiple cultures and age groups... and we found that EVERYONE has a similar vision of the Ideal Working Environment. These were the 5 elements.

      § Teamwork – people work together to achieve objectives even if they may go in different directions they communicate and give each other feedback so everyone wins

      § Trust – the ability to be trusted to do your job in your own way and express your talents and ideas to solve problems... or knowing someone will help you to achieve your goals. Know that people are taking accountability for their objectives and you don't need to worry.

§ Clarity – communication, vision, feedback that supports an understanding of what to do, where to go and who to do it with so everyone can succeed

§ A Supportive Environment – knowing that the boss will actually listen to you, that the head of finance will try to understand your budget issues, or that policies can be modified in unforeseen circumstances.

§ Fun – well… fun

o By getting the people to come up with their own Ideal Working Environment, you will find this same predictable outcome.

– Showing that the Time the game requires will be recovered in other areas with higher productivity and cooperation.

And once you create awareness of the benefits, there will be obstacles… but these obstacles will mostly be an illusion. What are they? The Enemy!

The enemy is important in leadership. It is used in wars, espionage, politics, marketing and naturally, the legal profession. The idea is as old as humanity. You have uncooperative tribes (departments) that are primarily concerned with their own thing and may even fight from time to time. Suddenly, a larger enemy appears that threatens them all. Upon discovery of this bigger enemy, the tribes (departments), pool together to fight against the bigger enemy. Through this effort, they form bonds and create supportive relationships that last past the crisis.

So who is the enemy?

The easiest enemy to find is an actual advisory. People who are out to kill the "Ideal Work Environment"… people who believe that work should be hard and NOT FUN!!! Those vicious individuals who get satisfaction from being stressed out and seeing others stressed out too. THEY ARE THE ENEMY!

There are three things we can do with the enemy:

1.   Eliminate them – the most drastic and yet most effective of all strategies because it not only gets rid of a negative influence but also sends a message to others, that coming together as a "Family" to create a great environment will not tolerate "Destroyers of Fun"

2.   Make the Enemy your friend – this is the most practical solution but not the easiest. It requires patience and vigilance to make sure there is more positive influence from multiple sides than the negative influencer can dish out. Otherwise, if the negative influencer is too powerful, they could

engulf much of the work you have done, and you lose the game.

      a. In an organizational culture change initiative we did for the 3rd largest globally GRP pipe manufacturer based in Iran, the brother of the owner, Hamid, was totally against this New Psychology stuff! He would fly off to Dubai or Istanbul specifically to avoid being part of the project... and everyone knows he needed it the most. After the initiative, Hamid did not participate or acknowledge any of the changes the people had and were implementing. While the company-wide efforts were still in play by his brother the CEO, he would not join. But during this whole time, 7 subordinates were constantly working on him. Five months after the initiative finally he started to participate. While only a bit, in the beginning, it was a huge triumph for the whole group and the entire organization rallied to support getting him onboard. Within a month, he was not only participating fully and being a positive influence... but actually having fun in the process.

3.   Create a Special "Happy Department" – This is for those who cannot be Eliminated but need to be separated. This solution takes extra resources but

may prove to have an additional bonus.

a. An organizational Culture Initiative with the Malaysian Government presented a challenge: they could not fire anyone. Unfortunately, the division we were working with had a larger than usual number of negative influencers. The solution turned out to be quite positive. We created a Happy Department where negative influencers regardless of their rank and pay grade, were kept with the sole purpose of finding and promoting individuals in the company who were adding value to the culture and consistently living the behaviors that were set by their peers through the gamification efforts. They were angry in the beginning and some resigned (problem solved) but there were still some Hardcore Villains that were going to stick it out no matter what.

b. The accidental rainbow… After a while, due to their required focus on all the things that supported a happier culture and positive outcomes… and the recognition of the people who achieved them… many of the angry villains became advocates. This solution ultimately became a preference, but the initiation was painful due to the MASSIVE resistance and anger shown by some of these people. While the results were "eventually" better, it took some resolve of the management to ride it out. Part of our role was making sure the management remained absolved of stripping these people of their significance, so the "blame" went to the consultants (us). Because removing negative influencers was part of the agreement, and negative influences were identified through interviewing the staff, and since there was no pay or benefit reduction, management was indemnified as part of securing the success of the culture initiative that was agreed in advance. So the relationships were maintained.

Leadership is not about getting people to follow you or do what you say, but the ability to create an environment that brings out the best in the people you lead. Gamification is a tool to create this type of environment. While it is ideal that "all" people will be a part of the grand scheme and prosper in the process, there will be an enemy, and uniting the rest of the people who "FIT" in your culture against this enemy is supporting the greater purpose of the organization. Great leaders will never be able to harmonize or please everyone, but they create GREAT opportunities for those who really matter in achieving an awesome organization.

And so how we structure our work gamification is essential for supporting the people with the right attitudes and eliminating those who have attitudes that may damage the others... The Enemy.

Creating Game Mechanics to WIN

S tructuring the game is the key to success! After multiple attempts and lots of research, here are all 8 game stages that I find can be applied to any organizational objective. But I figure you will want some specific examples to apply too… so in this chapter, I have also included 5 scenarios and Game Mechanics that you can use, modify, or just appreciate.

Game mechanics

1. **Set the goals** – goals should be connected to outcomes that team members can achieve through the mental and/or physical resources they have. This could be intangible like an attitude, cross-departmental communication, or Innovation, or it could be specific results like a specific sales number, or specific customer service rating.

2. **Identify the behaviors required to achieve that goal** – identify the specific behaviors that support the achievement of the goals. Find high performers for this explicit goal and identify the specific behaviors, attitudes, and even values that support their success in achieving it.

3. **Identify the emotional drives that will motivate those behaviors** – each behavior has a set of motivators that reinforce consistency and action. These are the 8 Emotional Drives discussed earlier, and there are usually 2 or 3 drivers that you can identify with a little thought, that support the behaviors you have chosen. Each emotional drive

also correlates to various game structures. See these
below

4. **Create a Theme to connect everything** – this will
be a team effort and should have some consensus. If
you like superheroes but half your team does not…
they will not be excited by the theme for the game.
So, it is important to find something that "most"
people can agree to. I say "most" because sometimes
you may find one individual who just hates
everything and the amount of time and frustration
trying to please this type of person negatively affects
the ENTIRE team… so work with the people who
like fun!

    a. Here are some questions to ask about your
Theme:

        i. What are the journey goals?

        ii. Is there any fantasy mixed?

        iii. Why do players go on the journey?

        iv. What types of obstacles will they
face?

        v. Is there one continuous journey or
are there many small ones?

        vi. Who are the characters of the story?

        vii. Do you have avatars?

        viii.   Do you have special powers?

        ix.   Can you get special powers through achievement?

        x.   Are there teams, individuals or both?

b. If teams, do you have flags or special identifying banners

        i.   Where does the story happen?

        ii.   Where does it begin?

        iii.   Where does it end?

The theme is the element that supports diversity and makes the effort more fun. People get to be someone else, as an avatar, you can have more power of achievement and possibly live up to the challenge because you have stepped out of the limitations created by reality.

5. Design the game structure – Structure Elements can be combined based on the game objectives, the requirements of who needs to be involved, the required behaviors, and the Emotional Drives that motivate those behaviors. All of these built around the game theme.

Structure Elements that work for the activities that should be measured and rewarded, then connect them to make a fun and motivating flow that will be the foundation of the gamified work process. These game elements could be quests where your team must complete a larger goal with a number of smaller achievements (milestones), and avoid obstacles that hinder your goals… or a goal-focused competition where competing teams require cooperation in acquiring resources to achieve the goal.

Game structures can be modularized based on the desired outcome of the overall objective. Here are some examples:

a. Avoid Obstacles - A defined negative outcome or behavior that is awarded or rewarded if avoided.

b. Cooperation - The requirement to cooperate with other team members or departments or vendors to achieve a specific result or environment.

c. Turns - One after the other, it's your turn to do the dishes or try your hand at a winning innovation. Each turn must-have criteria and an objective.

d. Transactions - When you need to get something done, you may need to establish a perimeter for transitions – the making of deals between 2 or more parties. Transactions can use various elements such as points, money, time…

e. Recourse acquisition - Acquiring things you need to achieve goals or support your team. A structured and measurable process to define or uncover what resources are needed and then acquire them with a specific purpose.

f. Special Teams - The grouping of people to do non-work-related efforts to support a cause or socially responsible effort from the company.

g. Competition - Competing to achieve, improve or support. Competitions are usually against other team members or departments.

h. Challenge - Can you achieve this target as a team or individual? A challenge is not against another team or individual a goal or against personal bests. It can include amounts saved, speed of achievement, personal improvement in productivity.

i. Quests - Finding the best process... or getting that one special customer... this will require multiple actions usually by multiple people to achieve it.

>   i. i.e. creating the ultimate team productivity or the ideal work environment

j. Combat - A specific competition on an event that happens at a specific time between 2 or more people.

>   i. i.e. The finance and the procurement teams have a dispute, so they have combat between the 2 department heads to see who can convince the Operations head on the right procedure.

>   ii. i.e. at the end of the month, 2 team members are tied for #1, so they must each spend one day to see who can make the most sales in an 8-hour period.

>   iii. i.e. if an argument breaks out, the 2 parties must have combat with foam swords and then sit

down to solve the problem with the winner having the advantage

k. WIN STATE - Win state is the clear definition of what a team or individual has done or achieved to be considered a winner.

6. **Design the Rewards related to "Win State"** – Ask the questions: Who wins? How do they win? How many wins? What do they get when they win? What do they feel when they win? What do they need to have to win? The win state can also connect to the emotional drives you are supporting. For example, if the behaviors are supported by the emotional drive of contribution, Win state may include collections to support a local charity or group requiring assistance. If the primary emotional drive is Belonging/Love, having a team or company party may be a better Win State than individual rewards. If Recognition is a key motivator to achieve objectives, then showing the winners' pictures and achievements will be more effective. Win state is about filling the EMOTIONS related to the successful application of the behaviors required to achieve objectives. Some of these rewards may include:

a. Achievement Recognition - To show an individuals or team's Achievements publicly

    i.   i.e. A team banner is displayed if they win a weekly competition

> ii.   i.e. An individual's picture is posted on the wall after an achievement
>
> iii.   i.e. A star is placed on a chart with people's pictures

b. Badges - To show the achievement of a level or accumulation of points. Badges can be physical or virtual

> i.   i.e. A team or individual is awarded a Badge of Communication Ninja as recognition for accumulating 20 points in cross-department communication

c. Gifting - To give a gift or reward to others as a form of contribution for the efforts and achievement of an individual or team.

> i.   i.e. The team achieves a sales goal and the company donated 10 computers to a local school.

d. Points - To collect points based on actions, achievements, support, or efforts.

> i.   i.e. team member receives 5 points when they achieve a goal
>
> ii.   i.e. team member earns black 1 point when they are late
>
> iii.   i.e. after a team member has 50 points they reach a new level or get a badge

e. Collections - Collections are based on positive or

negative behaviors or results. They can be collected for the team or for external charity and be anything from money to canned food.

    i.   i.e. Team members pay $1 every time they are late and the collections are used for a monthly outing.

    ii.   i.e. team members donate as they please for an internal recreation room and the company will match the donation when a goal is reached.

f. Team Unity - The creation flags, t-shirts, banners, button, or wearing specific colors to maintain a unified team identity. This can also be connected with levels or badges

    i.   i.e. when an individual reaches a level of productivity, he is awarded as part of elite Productivity Ninjas and is allowed the black ninja t-shirt as part of the elite team

    ii.   i.e. the R&D team has their banner posted on the wall because they were the winning performers for the week over the other department teams

g. Levels - A set of stages a team or team member can advance as part of an accumulation of points, badges, achievements, usually with the theme…

    i.   i.e. when a team member accumulates 20

points or collects 2 badges, he advances to the level of Super Hero

ii.   i.e. after the team member reaches the 4th level of Black Knight, he is allowed to unlock the chest that contains the mystery lunch package for

h. Tangible Rewards - A reward for an achievement or accumulation that could be money, a new office, better tools...

i.   i.e. after unlocking 8 parts of the combination lock through various achievements and levels, a team or team member accesses a $1000 bonus

ii.   i.e. each new level achieved comes with a badge and a $100 reward

i. Content Unlocking - A complete result that is broken down into parts so that each part can be "unlocked" when an achievement, or level, or number of points is reached.

i.   i.e. 8 movie tickets are in a box and it is hidden so that you must have a treasure map to find it. The map is broken into 4 pieces and each team must achieve their weekly goal to get a piece. When all the pieces are found, they can find the ticket and have a fun day at the movies.

For game mechanics and rewards, emotional drives also play an important role. If you have identified the Emotional Drives for each behavior, then specific types of structures work better than others. Here are the emotional drives and some examples of the mechanics and rewards that support them.

Structures, activities, and game elements that support working together with others, teamwork, supporting others, and collaboration… provide gratification of the Emotional Drive of Love & Belonging

BELONGING / LOVE

Connection from being with others or sense with self

Structures, activities, and game elements that provide clarity, and a personal sense of control or direction... provide gratification of the Emotional Drive of Security and Control

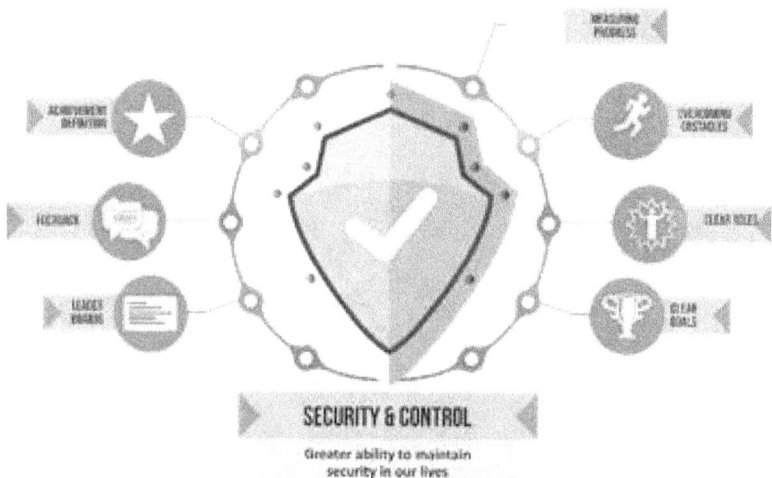

Structures, activities, and game elements that create a different environment, uncommon activities, unique opportunities, or anything outside of the scope of normal, or usual... provide gratification of the Emotional Drive of Diversity & Change

Structures, activities, and game elements that show the accomplishments and value a person is adding to the team or organization through their ideas or efforts... provide gratification of the Emotional Drive of Recognition & Change.

RECOGNITION/ SIGNIFICANCE

Doing something notable and getting
I sense of personal value

Structures, activities, and game elements that help people feel they have completed something, finished a part so they can move to the next part, or show progress in their efforts provide gratification of the Emotional Drive of Achievement.

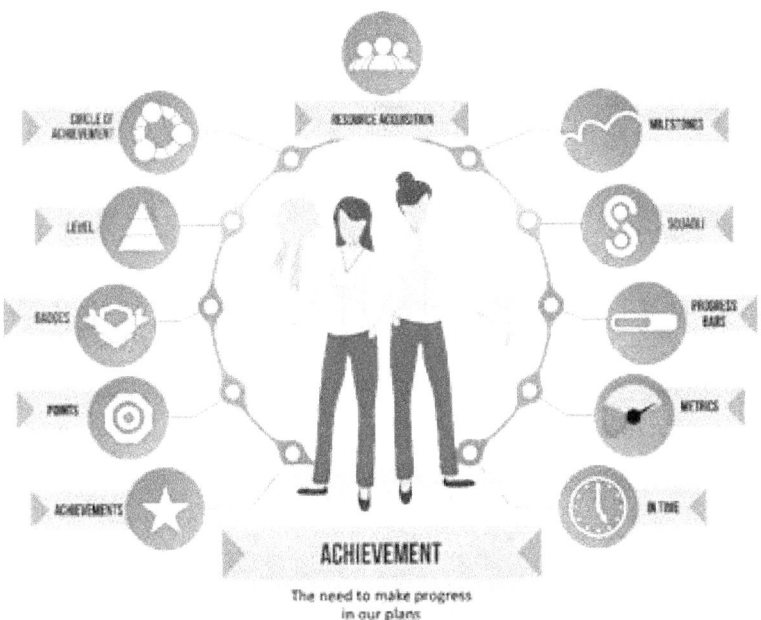

Structures, activities, and game elements that support learning, personal improvement, or challenging existing abilities... provide gratification of the Emotional Drive of Challenge & Growth.

Structures, activities, and game elements that support a personal sense of pride in the level of quality of actions, creations, or achievements... provide gratification of the Emotional Drive of Excellence

Structures, activities, and game elements that provide a means by which to help or support others, to give to those who have less than you do, or create more happiness or achievement in people's lives... provide gratification of the Emotional Drive of Responsibility & Contribution

RESPONSIBILITY/CONTRIBUTION

The need to contribute

7. **Identify game partners** – The most obvious players are our team, but what if we include people, teams, organizations that support us. Game Partners could be vendors and even customers. Getting others involved expands not only expands the scope of the game but the accountability in standard and achievement.

   a. Here are some questions you can ask to identify Partners:

      i. What type of partners do you need? Why?

      ii. What do you need from a partner to succeed?

      iii. What should a partner need from you to succeed?

      iv. What must each partner have to keep consistent and achieve mutual objectives?

      v. What emotional drives should be common in the partnership?

      vi. How will partners fit into the game?

      vii. What are the results each partner will see?

8. **Measure Everything**: Connect, report, and promote measurement of the game outcomes – Measurement and the display of measurement is the key to successful gamification. Knowing how you do in a specific

behavior or achievement and when you are on track provides clarity and confidence. While Squadli is a powerful tool to measure and gamify the measurement should be in the physical world as well. Here are some ways to make if visible and make it fun:

a. Leaderboards - A display that shows the progress toward an objective of multiple teams or individuals at the same time to show who is in the lead and who is behind

b. Hero's Index - A display either physical or virtual of individuals or teams who have achieved a specific achievement or level

c. Progress Indicators - This measures one specific objective and the progress that is made towards it by teams or individuals

d. Time - A deadline to an objective or achievement

e. Milestones - Specific parts of a bigger objective that can be celebrated or rewarded

f. Finish Line - Is this a continuous process or is there a defined finish?

Here are five scenarios we applied for clients that will give some insights to see these in action.

Scenario 1 – a manufacturing company wants to improve morale and quality

Game: Transformers Saving the Earth with (Brand)

Teams involved in playing: manufacturing team, pre-production team, procurement team, finance team, marketing team

Key behaviors: Innovation, Excellence, Cooperation, Fun, No Blame.

Emotional Drives supporting behaviors: Growth, Diversity, Love & Belonging, Achievement

Mechanics:

Getting the Allspark (Transformer reference to what makes Transformers alive). This is the foundation and strength of each individual participating in the game. the Allspark determines whether you are in the game or not and the only way to get Allspark "Energon" is through cooperation within and across departments. The Allspark comes from human connection. The behaviors of cooperation, internal support, respect of other's time, and basic kindness are rewarded with "Energon". Likewise, no cooperation, being unkind, disrespecting other's time, or no support will result in negative Energon.

Allspark Energon is allocated to the individual but is also consolidated for teams. Positive or negative Energon is given by observing managers, peers, and subordinates. Manager Energon distribution is also counted and added up to determine team scores.

As individuals increase in Energon, he evolves to higher ranking transformers. If the individual decreases in Energon, they are stripped of rank.

The more Hi Ranking Transformers a Team has, the more power and life force it can attain at the bi-monthly Transformer team fights where the teams will have physical Nerf style fights. More life force means you can be hit more time and still survive. Winning teams will get a trophy till the next fight.

The game also supports the different teams of (brand) in the process from design to the end sale, teams get weapon awards they can use to win the competition.

Manufacturing team – The team has zero defects and timely output

R&D and pre-production team – the team works with the marketing, procurement, and manufacturing team to create high performing products

Procurement team – searches and shares possible material and new advances to support innovation of products

finance team – quickly supports and approves budgets within policy or adjusts policy to market requirements if necessary, to ensure time to market and on-time procurement

marketing team – involves other teams in brainstorming and works with idea originators in creating winning campaigns

Innovation rewards come from cross-departmental cooperation in finding new ways to design, build and manufacture

Rewards and Win State:

Positive and negative Energon is distributed through Energon points. Every 2 months the points start over to make sure everyone has an opportunity. An individual evolves or devolves to a new rank at intervals of 20 Energon points. There are 5 levels of evolution and maximum evolution is to a (Brand) Prime. The more Energon, the better the chance for the Transformer Team to win and the team to have the achievement.

Measurement:

Energon points are given through Squadli

Each Prime Transformer Team is listed in the hall of heroes. Individuals who participate in the transformer fights are listed in the org chart of wins and achievements with their pictures.

Scenario 2 – a financial institution wants to be more innovative, improve market share and reduce bad debt with digital transformation

Game: (Brand) Wizards from the Gold Zone

Teams involved in playing: front line team, product development team, debt collection team, marketing team

Key behaviors: Innovation, proactive action, Cooperation, Fun, No Blame

Emotional Drives supporting behaviors: Growth, Recognition, Achievement

Mechanics:

Turning Gold into Magic. The wizard's power of magic depends on 3 factors:

1. how much gold they have

2. how many other wizards are supporting the spell

3. the size of the financial impact

Innovative processes, products, or marketing to support more market share or less bad debt are used to create a spell. The wizard who initiates the idea will get 2 gold bars for every idea that is backed. They are put up on the wizard's choice board. Wizards (team members) choose what spells they want to back. If there are at least 5 wizards from any relevant team or department, spell is activated. If a wizard backs a spell they also get 1 gold bar.

They build the spell (idea) and present it in the Sphere of Magic held every 2 months where other wizards vote on the practical implementation of the spell. When a wizard votes for a spell, they are backing it. Only the best and most practical spells are adopted and get the most wizards behind it. Each spell that is backed at the Sphere of Magic provides 3 gold bars to each of the presenting wizards and 6 to the originating wizard.

If the spell is implemented and has success, each wizard is rewarded with 1 gold bar for every $10,000 (or relevant amount) of revenue or cost savings. The wizard who originated the spell gets 2 gold bars for every $10,000 of revenue or cost-saving.

Wizards can use the gold bars to buy items online. Like:

- Be boss wizard for a day

- Magic to win arguments

- Magic to travel

- Magic to win Favours

Wizards can consolidate gold to have:

- magic parties

- high-level dinners

- magic team trips

By giving people the opportunity to join and support others rather than everyone competing against each other, only the high potential projects get supported and the use of time to innovation is more practically allocated. This also supports cross-departmental cooperation and collaboration because innovation implementation will usually require multiple departments to succeed... and everyone likes to be on a winning team... and now, the team is a multi-department team, so silos are largely eliminated.

Rewards and Win State:

Every team that had backers can be recognized at some level at the Sphere of Magic and at the end of the year Wizards Ball. Each wizard who has achieved 10 gold bars gets promoted to master wizard and those who achieve 30 are grandmaster wizards. Grandmaster Wizards get to be on the panel for deciding the main spells to pursue.

Measurement:

Gold bars are given through a digital leader board that shows all the different "Spells", the originators and the team who backs them with their pictures.

Awards are given at the Sphere of Magic and at the Wizards Ball.

Scenario 3 – a telecommunications company feels its employees have become complacent and wants to improve productivity, service, and proactive leadership

Game: Escaping the Zombie Virus

Teams involved in playing: Service team, C-suite, finance team, marketing team, public relations team, field teams, concept development team

Key behaviors: Proactive leadership, Caring, Cooperation, Fun, No Blame, high energy

Emotional Drives supporting behaviors: Growth, Recognition, Love & Belonging, Achievement

Mechanics:

An epidemic has broken out and employees are turning into zombies. There is a cure but prevention has the best results since once you are a zombie you need to be in quarantine for a month.

Zombie symptoms are:

- No new ideas

- low energy

- low initiative

- waiting for people to tell you what to do

- unsupportive

- Indifferent to others

Since the zombie virus can infect anyone or even an entire team, there is no blame or penalty for zombie behavior, but there are rewards for curing zombies evolving humans. But being aware that Zombie behavior is infectious, teams need to build up their zombie vaccine points to survive.

Immunity vaccine points can be earned by identifying consistent zombie behaviors in team members and supporting their recovery. If an individual or a team identify zombie behaviors, they become the zombie hunters to support zombie recovery. Individuals and teams who are successful are awarded. Teams may have a "DON'T EAT MY BRAIN" sign to discourage zombie behavior.

Individual Awards

- Evolved Human (20 points) consistent high positive energy that infects others and is applied to proactive execution of decisions and ideas. Evolved humans get their picture on the hall of heroes at the top

- Extraordinary Human (15 points) consistent proactive execution of decisions and ideas

- Zombie Warrior (12 points) 5 humans saved

- Prevent a Zombie – caring leadership (10 points) must remain human for 30 days

- Cure a Zombie – leadership (8 points) must remain human for 30 days after cure

- Zombie Recovery – self-leadership (5 points) must remain human for 30 days

Team Awards

- No Zombie Zone Award (50 points) the entire team must be zombie-free for the entire month

- Zombie Warrior Team Award (50 points) supporting other teams and individuals to be zombie-free (total 20 humans saved)

The Anti-zombie central command verifies the zombie recovery and the zombie-free zones to ensure integrity. They may also identify zombies and find leaders to support them. Central command can also be scrutinized if zombie hunters see zombie behaviors in them as well.

Measurement:

Anti-zombie central command, teams, and individuals all provide regular feedback to each other using Squadli (the desired behaviors are set as the objectives in the system).

Every zombie behavior is a negative point of emoji. Depending on the severity, it could be from -1 to -3 (negative points reduce immunity and affect team immunity). These behaviors must be referenced as the reduction of one of the Behavior Objectives (i.e. the desired objective of "caring" is countered by the zombie behavior of being indifferent). Being diagnosed with zombie behavior does not affect the individual exhibiting it (after all, they are just infected), but it does affect that person's team since they should support them in achieving zombie-free status. Customer complaints are also recognized as negative points on the separate External Scale

Every immunity vaccine behavior is a positive point emoji. Depending on the power, it could be from +1 to +3 (positive points support individual and team immunity). These key behaviors are also referenced when giving emoji. Customer praise is also recognized as positive points on the separate External Scale

Rewards and Win State:

The game resets at the end of every month. Zombie hunters, Evolved and Extraordinary Humans, and Zombie free teams are rewarded with small trophies and have their pictures on the hall of warriors.

At the end of the quarter, if the organization immunity reaches +500 points, the company has a Zombie party where the evolved humans lead the organization (with support of other volunteers)

Scenario 4 – a university has become less competitive due to more innovative education in more updated institutions and wants to regain its competitive advantage.

Game: [Brand] Heroes of Awesomeness

Teams involved in playing: Students, Teachers, Administrators, Marketing

Key behaviors: Supportive, Innovative, Fun, Learning, Cooperative, Coaching

Emotional Drives supporting behaviors: Growth, Recognition, Achievement, Diversity, Belonging

Mechanics:

Humanity has created a world of Mediocrity. People are being assimilated into a society of mediocrity. But a new group of rebel heroes is fighting against the powers of ordinary people which will lead to the ultimate doom of humanity. [Brand] has assembled the heroes of the future who will shift the potential of civilization to a brighter future and create a brave new world of where people live and work at their potential and life is Awesome.

To achieve this, they must work together to bring out the best in each other and lead the revolution of greatness. They have created 6 hives and (including one for the school staff) each hive has individual pods of selected heroes who complement each other's powers. Pods have unique identities created by their members and each member takes a turn to lead the pod in learning and implementing new ideas and reinventing old ones.

Each of the hives represent different factions: Thinkers, Futurists, Gradians, Explorers, Warriors and Coaches (the teachers/professors). While all are working towards a better future, they do have friendly competitions. Yet there are times when they must all work together to achieve higher objectives.

There are 3 levels of competition.

The first is at the Pod level within the Hive. Each pod has its own identity, mission, and name and collects points for various areas of excellence and behaviors. Pods compete in the following areas:

- Academic achievement

- Leadership within the Hive

- Social media following (Pod YouTube Channels where they teach what they learn)

- Presentation and influence

- Teach others to Master curriculum (because the students take on the role of teacher and the teacher takes on the role of coach to support the students to teach each other... they are not measured on their own academics but on how well they help others improve... which ultimately affects their own)

- Implementation of innovation

- Thought leadership

- Book sales (individuals will write a book related to their studies and Pod members support in editing, publishing, and marketing)

The Hive has its own colors and the pods incorporate these colors to create their own identity. The collective Pods work together to support the Hive. Hives compete in the following areas:

- Sports

- Consolidated Academic achievement

- Impact on community

- Total number of Book Sales (from all Pods)

- Hive businesses run by rotation in roles from the Pods

The Collective competes against the standards and the established norms. They look at achievements rather than grades and identify areas of business and thought leadership to establish benchmarks.

Measurement:

PODS

Pod level leadership, thought leadership, collaborative, innovative, teaching performance, and supportive behaviors are measured through Squali. Points are given from administrators, coaches and hive leaders based on the exhibition of the predefined behaviors of individuals which are added to create

Pod scores. Pod level behaviors are scored in positive and negative emoji from -3 to +3 and weekly awards may be given to reflect results from those behaviors. Awards range from +5 points to +10, they are:

- Thought Leader award

- Teacher/coach award

- Leadership award

- Innovation award

- Super support award

- Influence and presentation award

- Best HIVE books

- Best HIVE teaching channel

HIVES

The Hives are measured by administrators and coaches. As each hive is a collective of Pods, the behaviors and performance of the Pods affect the overall Hive scores. Some of the other measures include:

- Top shows measured on subscribers, likes, and reviews.

- Books are measured on purchases and reviews

Hives also have students run businesses where profit is distributed to the students who run them. profitability is also a measure that comes with its own reward.

THE COLLECTIVE

The Collective combines Pods and Hives to measure them against industry norms. Pods exceeding the norms achieve awards of being Heroes of Awesomeness. Hives who have more than 5 successful Pods achieve the Hero Maker awards.

Rewards and Win State:

Each Pod and Hive have opportunities to win in different categories thus perpetuating the motivation across the entire collective. Individuals are rewarded through the Pods and Hives. Measures are being created consistently and are tabulated weekly to put on the Hero Index boards. The weekly results are tabulated again for each school quarter, and then again for each end of the school year. The top Pods (from various categories) in a Hive are awarded Hero awards at the Heroes Gala where members of each Hive wear hive colors and represent their unique Pods in

Scenario 5 – A Hotel wishes to create extraordinary service

Game: Diamond Hunters of [Brand]

Teams involved in playing: service staff (front of the house), room cleaners, kitchen staff, engineers (back of the house)

Key behaviors: Guest focused, Supportive, Innovative, Fun, Caring, Creating "Wow" Experiences, Teamwork

Emotional Drives supporting behaviors: Recognition,

Achievement, Excellence, Belonging

Mechanics:

Each guest has a hidden Diamonds that can be found through extreme positive emotions, which can only be achieved through personalized, creative experiences. But each guest is different so what works for one, may not work for another. It is the mission of the team to discover these hidden diamonds by finding a unique way to elicit WOW experiences from each guest.

Both front and back of the house teams and individuals compete to find ways to break the code for each guest that supports extraordinary experience. The value of the uncovered Diamond is based on 5 factors.

1.   Mentions to the management

2.   Mentions in social media

3.   Reviews Rating

4.   Reviews Quality

5.   Personal Recommendations

As individuals and teams play, they achieve points and Diamonds to determine the Diamond Hunter ranks. There are 4 Ranks of excellence that can be attained each month. They are:

1.   Digger

2.   Geo Navigator

3.   Diamond hunter

4.   Master Diamond hunter

Guests are also encouraged to be part of the game and support staff if and when they uncover diamonds throughout their stay.

Measurement:

Teams and individuals are rated on the behaviors and innovation related to creating WOW moments. We use Squadli to measure diamond hunter value.

- Points are distributed through Emoji -3 to +3 for behaviors

- Diamond awards based on the value of uncovered Diamond

Behavior points are given by management based on the following criteria:

- Active guest focus – **1 point** (being supportive and attentive)

- Opportunistic diamond extraction - **2 points** (discovering a way for

- Innovative planned diamond extraction - **3 points**

Diamond awards are given for specific results (5 behavior points = 1 Diamond Award)

- Mentions to the management: **1 diamond**

- Mentions in social media: **2 diamonds** per specific

service-related mention

- Reviews Rating – **3 diamonds** for 5 stars (10/10) with specific service-related mention

- Reviews Quality – **4 diamonds** for 5 stars (10/10) with specific service-related description

- Personal Recommendations – **5 diamonds** for specific referral based on service

The Diamonds and points can be for an individual or a team. While an individual will gain more personal benefit, they stand to get more bonuses if they work together. This also creates a sense of accountability because if one or 2 individuals are getting most of the points, they might as well do it alone if team members do not support. At the beginning of each month, all staff starts at the rank of "Digger".

- Digger (below 1 diamond)

- Geo Navigator (1 to 2 diamonds)

- Diamond hunter (3 to 5 diamonds)

- Master Diamond hunter (More than 5 diamonds)

Each new month is a clean slate. At the end of the month, all diamonds are reclaimed and must be cashed in.

Bonuses: any individual or team who makes 25 diamonds in one month gets an extra 10 diamonds.

Rewards and Win State:

Diamonds can be exchanged for cash and prizes at the end of the month. Each month, badges for Diamond Hunter and Master Diamond Hunter are given out for staff to wear on their uniform if they have been earned. And cash and prizes are given

The best way to create a fun, relevant and practical game is by getting the staff themselves to create the gamified work processes. Management and HR will also need to be involved for the rewards and recognition, tying game results to other compensation and benefits and maintaining the integrity of the game. In the next chapter, we put it together to show how all this affects organizational culture in a big way!

Achieving the Ultimate Organizational Culture

Ｗe start with passion, innovation, and excitement when we begin a job. When the diversity wears out, the diminished sense of personal value kicks in, and the environment doesn't support the greater you… you become a victim of "organizational culture atrophy". But now we are armed with the weapons of psychology, fun, and awareness, we are ready to take on the giant beast that plagues us and the people we work with. We are ready to build an EXTRAORDINARY organizational culture from the power of imagination and the intimate desire to stay a child.

We must first set our strategy

1. Do a culture audit, using the Culture Evolution Assessment tool is a fast and inexpensive way to find out where you are before plotting a course to where you want to be. The Tool can be found at: www.cultureevolution.com

   a. As a part of the culture audit, do an organizational communication process audit using the Colored Brain tool. This also identifies one of the root causes of why trust breaks down. Find more about the Colored Brain system at: www.coloredbrain.com

   b. Find management perception gaps using the Management Mirror EDMA tool. This identifies the difference between how management sees themselves compared to how others see them. And since most managers want to be good leaders, this will help them understand what strategies are not working to be the type of leader they think they are.

c. Ask the people what they want to change. This is best done with an independent party with the surety that information will be kept confidential. But it can be achieved with between 15% to 40% of the organization being interviewed using these 2 questions:

   i.   If you were the CEO, what would you change in the organization?

   ii.   What are your biggest frustrations working here?

These are actually the same question but different people will react to them differently and give you some amazing data. When you tabulate the data you will find that there are 3 to 5 changes that most people want... these are areas to focus on as a Fun Change Initiative.

Find the Key influencers – the people who others highly respect and trust. These people may be the tea lady of the guy who's always cracking jokes but whoever they are, you need to identify them so they can help you implement the gamification and culture evolution. This is possible to determine in the interviews by simply asking people who are the two or three people they respect and trust the most.

2. Work with the key influencers to get feedback from their

circle of influence to define how these 3 to 5 changes connect to the direction of culture you want to evolve to and the Ideal Work Environment (as mentioned in the "Choosing the Leader Avatar" Chapter).

3. Define the results, skills, and attitudes required to create these changes and the Ideal Work Environment.

4. Help the key influencers define the behaviors or guiding principles required to achieve the results, skills, and attitudes. Support them with time and brainstorming sessions so they can get others involved.

5. Define the emotional Drives that support those behaviors.

6. Get together with influencers and create a Game Theme based feedback they get from their circle of influence. Remember to create diversity and be interesting enough for most people to get interested.

7. Kick out "The Enemy" if they appear

8. Work with influencers and stakeholders to create the game mechanics and basic structure

9. Work with the Communications, PR, Admin, and/or HR departments plus management to get the structure implemented

10. Get agreement on what, how, and when of the game rewards… plus any tangible rewards associated with the game and the game rewards

11. Find partners to play with. The teams and departments are not the only potential players. Think globally... How can you get customers and vendors involved? How could your clients or vendors be included to achieve the results and objectives you want?

12. Measure and display the behaviors or guiding principles in line with the theme and structure. Make sure it is clear what rewards are received with each defined measurement.

13. Re-measure the culture evolution using the OCEAN tool after 2 months. Share the improvements with the people and celebrate. This can be done 2 months later again to maintain continuous improvement.

14. Games get boring if you play too long, revisit the game theme and structure after 3 months or possibly even 2 months to coincide with the re-measurement. Create something new or modify existing to continue the newness.

Here is a summary of how all this will build a passionate, exciting and competent organizational culture

Work gamification Definition: Work gamification is about positive motivation structures created to consistently trigger and maintain excitement and interest in applying personal talents and innovation for the achievement of organizational goals... and enjoy it.

Start at the beginning... the first few weeks of work at a new company. Do you remember how excited you were? The possibilities, the plans, the POTENTIAL!

People are passionate and excited when there is hope.

Don't forget the motivational factor of "Feeling" valued. Not to be confused with recognition, but the instinct that your presence there makes a difference... and therefore supports a purpose. The measurement of social approval has always been a foundation of a personal sense of value, and in this PFB era, it has been digitized and supercharged.

Personal validation (like what we get from the gamified social media) is a way for us to measure our personal sense of value. Regardless of how much self-confidence we have, or how much or how little we care about what people think...

...and since value is connected to purpose... if we feel valuable, we feel like our lives have more purpose... which creates more "happiness" ...at least for a moment!

The 8 fundamental elements that must be in place before we begin work gamification structures are:

1. There must be an objective with a defined result

2. The result must apparently clear

3. You must believe the result will benefit you

4. You must believe you can achieve the result

5.   The process to achieve the result should be in line with your primary motivators

6.   You must be involved in the design of the process

7.   The process should not be counter to your elemental genetic "Ambiguity Relief" process.

8.   There must be clearly defined milestones that can be easily identified and measured when you achieve them.

Add the 8 elements to the 3 gamification criteria:

1.   Measurement

2.   Competition

3.   Story or theme

Feeling the Potential to Achieve is more important and longer-lasting motivator than actual achievement. When we create gamified processes that build up the individual's sense of potential, we build up the engagement and the ultimate result achieved in the process. This is shared in the **Gamification Value Perception Index** which includes:

Challenge: Rank Ascension that is but attainable is the key to maintaining confidence and interest. The moment someone feels they can't get to the next level, they give up.

Anticipation: anticipation keeps performers who have potential but are not at their achieving, motivated.

Validation: measurement and awards support validation of value an individual offers... as long as it's not too easy.

Comparison: the gap of comparison is directly related to the validation of value. Who/what are you comparing to affects the value of the validation... i.e. compared to best performer or to personal best performance?

Potential: some success ignites the Potential for Bigger success

Culture transformation is just like any game, you need to know where you are before you can begin your journey. There are 5 Levels of Culture Evolution that can be measured through the OCEAN culture tool at: www.cultureevolution.com

- The Blame Culture

- The Multi-Directional Culture

- The Live and Let Live Culture

- The Brand Congruent Culture

- The Leadership Enriched Culture

The enemies of fun are the enemies of engagement.

Fun comes from being OUT of the ordinary. When a situation is new, outside of our current day to day routine, we fill our emotional drive for Diversity and Change. And, how much diversity a person is willing to act on is subject to the importance or ranking of their emotional drive of Security and Control. When the **Fear Tolerance** is less than the fulfillment of the Diversity drive combined with other drives, fun changes to fear. The higher the need for Security, the more risk an action seems to have.

Repositioning Fear Tolerance to create Trust

Trust is a product of feeling safe, the absence of fear when interacting with others. But, when others do not understand us or try to push a process on us that we feel is not supporting our success, fear is ignited because we feel our ability to add values is reduced.

One of the root causes of why trust breaks down is the brain's genetic, clarity getting Ambiguity Relief process. Trust starts with accepting that our process to get clarity is genetic and since it cannot be changed, it is easier to accept. To learn more about how Colored Brain affects trust, check out my **Colored Brain TEDx talk.**

Blame is the Trust Killer, the biggest villain in our story so we must create a NO BLAME ZONE. The first step in creating a No Blame zone is getting the sign at: www.NoBlame.zone The instructions are there too in case you don't want to reread the chapter on trust. Remember that the alternative to blame for building accountability and developing employees is Failing Intelligently.

Use "Active Trust" to build engagement... Actively trust someone... even if you don't trust them!

How measuring behaviors creates more Success Motivation without creating complacency

Measuring new or defined behaviors that can be achieved but still present a **Challenge,** will create **Anticipation** of **Potential** though **Comparison** of multiple successes, which support **Validation** and of the individual, which build a gamified Success Motivation strategy.

In my own group of over 540 DC Psychology Certified Trainers/Coaches across 19 countries, we measure the behaviors that support them to build their competencies and their businesses. But out of this group, only about 200+ are truly active. Using the Squadli app (www.squadli.com) we track 8 behaviors that will support 2 objectives.

1.   Being the best possible trainer/consultant they can be

2.   Making lots of money at it

Leading a work gamification initiative requires 4 factors:

1.   The gamified process must be created by the people who do the work

2.   Implementation requires action

3.   Be part of the fun

4.   Be visible

The Ideal work Environment across counties, cultures, age, position, and education usually includes:

- Teamwork

- Trust

- Clarity

- A Supportive Environment

- Fun

And this Ideal Work Environment can be used as a common Greater Purpose that everyone can buy into

Structuring the game is the key to success! Here are the 8 game stages that can be applied to any organizational objective:

1.   Set the goals

2.   Identify the behaviors required to achieve that goal

3.   Identify the emotional drives that will motivate those behaviors

4.   Create a Theme to connect everything

5.   Design the game structure

6.   Design the Rewards related to "Win State"

7.   Identify game partners

8.   Measure Everything

And finally, as the game wizard, you are a facilitator, the people should create, theme and implement the games to solve their problems. It's still ok to connect their problems with organizational objectives because both benefit from a more innovative more fulfilled and motivated workforce.

If you need help in the creation of an Employee led Work Gamification we have created a game that you can play with your people to facilitate them to create their own gamified work processes using all the methods we spoke of in this book.

You can see more at: www.futureofwork.fun

The only thing left is to keep it sustainable!

According to Dr Sanjeev Dixit, author of Plan C, leadership thinking and management mindset to focus and leverage on building, nurturing, and leveraging the Culture of the Organisation to achieve the desired outcomes & results. Plan C is much more impactful, profound, and strategic than Plan A (Action orientation for immediate & visible outcomes & results) and Plan B (Backup Orientation for risk management/mitigation)

How to leverage Plan C in achieving the desired outcomes across different types of set ups whether start-ups, Small scale enterprise, Medium Scale enterprise, Government bodies & organizations, Multinationals or large conglomerates.

The five main ingredients of leveraging Plan C are:

1. **Culture Vision:** Any growth journey of any entity begins with a well-articulated and sharp vision that answers "Why we are doing what we are doing" and "How we would like to visualize

ourselves". When it comes to defining Culture Vision, it highlights the purpose and kind of Culture one need to have to sustain the Business growth agenda. As a sample of Culture Vision **"Achieve sustainable profitable growth through Values, Performance, and Agile Culture" or "Consistent growth through Disruptive Culture".** Once key pillars of Culture is sharply defined by the Promoter, CEO, and the top management then it brings clarity to the organization regarding the Key focus areas besides critical success factors which will eventually create a vibrant well lubricated and high touch-oriented culture

2. **Culture Design:** A good Culture design is defining the blueprint of "How" of translating the Culture Vision into real & SMART (Specific, Measurable, Achievable, Realistic & Timebound) actions. **Culture Audit** to assess what is the current status/stage of Culture in the organization and what bottlenecks and strengths can be leveraged to smoothly move ahead.

Typically like any effective & efficient design, Culture design also encompasses closed-loop and full proof approach and based on TBR approach as elaborately discussed in Chapter 9. Primarily Trigger and Reinforcers for supporting Values oriented behaviors need to be articulated well at the design level. But the *first thing first which needs to be incorporated in the Culture design are **Values & Purpose of the Organisation as it will provide direction and road map for everybody to build a contextual culture (way of working) which impacts the Organisation's performance.***

Also, as part of Culture design, it is very critical for CEO, CHRO, CXOs, and employees to define their responsibilities and accountabilities in driving and sustaining the deployment of right behaviors associated with Company's Values further building the Culture. The CEO plays a more significant role than all others as if he/she fails to influence and lead from the front then Culture design goes for a toss and just becomes a "tick box" activity.

*As defined in the **Culture Vision** regarding the Key pillars of the culture, while finalizing the Culture design, it is very important to build the granular plan and strategic intent regarding how to realize and achieve the defined pillars. For example, if Performance is one of the pillars of the Culture then what all be done to ensure that there are Reinforcers defined to promote performance-driven behaviors.*

3.   ***Culture Actions:*** *In this stage of Plan C development, all the "How" part articulated in **Culture Design** is executed effectively and efficiently as per the given timeline. The Key of*

this stage success is high standard and level of execution with excellence. All great organizations excel in Culture Actions provided they had defined the previous two stages well. Any gap in the execution can short change the entire deliverables of Culture Actions. All the improvement & development plans derived out of Culture Audits also get well executed in this stage for bridging all the necessary gaps between current and desired stage.

4. **Culture Reviews:** *As part of Culture review, CEO and top management rigorously and in a disciplined manner monthly/quarterly review the progress of culture building plan execution against the identified review parameters.*

It can be done on over Balance Score Card review format or any simple format in terms of

1. *Improvement in Culture Audit score*

2. *Values deployment level*

3. *Triggers & Reinforcers*

4. *Planned actions vs actual %ages as*

5. *Employee engagement survey score improvement*

5. **Culture Improvements:** *This is the last stage of the continuous process of **Plan C** wherein all the*

*learnings from all the previous four stages are put for correction and this stage is primarily meant for continuous improvement of all stages of **Plan C**. All the gaps found gets addressed so that the desired culture takes shape and mature.*

Navigating the Sustainability Matrix

Games, restaurants, clubs and even relationships become Boring if left the same.

Like in relationships, new discoveries about each other, a few disagreements and making up, diversity in life through friends and work all add up to an improved relationship because they mix up the daily and weekly routine. But in a game, the structure and parameters are there and it's a daily thing...

Any gamification strategy should have a 3-month life span. If the same game and the same theme last too long, it will eventually get boring... but this is good news!

Since the groundwork is already done, and we have the measurement and can clearly see who the high performers are and why... we can simply reinvent this to do 3 things:

1. Improve the standards of achievement and results adding a little more challenge

2. Create a structure that supports the improvement of the lower achievers, so they also get more motivated.

3. It provides a platform to modify objectives according

to the state of the organization and its immediate issues

How to do it…

Make an event out of it, get everyone involved, have a pizza party, and set aside a day. 2 weeks before that have a contest for a theme and structure, then vote. Getting people involved will reinvigorate the ultimate buy into the game and the results the game should produce.

When making the game becomes a game, your people are getting all their most innovative potential and will come up with practical ideas to make work fun and productive. They get all the **Challenge, Anticipation, discovery of Potential,** and ultimately **Validation** while filling their Emotional Drives and feeling a sense of ownership. They will be ready to make things happen, they will be excited when you the Game Wizards raises his hands and says GAME ON!

PANDEMIC READY CULTURE GAMIFICATION STRATEGIES

The COVID19 pandemic has transformed business and has drastically affected culture. The uncertainty, isolation, and in many cases salary reduction has caused disruption in many people's lives. However, the pandemic has also created a unique opportunity to improve morale AND improve culture where it may have been more difficult before.

Many organizations aspire to do some type of culture evolution but have not moved on it, or have done training or short term initiatives in hopes of improving their culture. Initiatives that are usually temporary quick fixes that do not affect the root cause problem. But the biggest issue is not the investment required in a root case culture evolution project, it's the time and potential productivity loss of such a project without any real guarantee of ROI.

But in the wake of the pandemic, employees' time constraints and focus has changed, leaving new opportunities to build better, more engaging organizational cultures virtually to affect the overall wellness of the organization and its ultimate competitiveness in a disruptive New Normal environment.

Enter gamification to recover employee optimism, energy, innovation, and purpose in a disruptive environment...

A key factor in the success of a more excited group with the ability to solve problems is HUMAN CONNECTION... and a gamification strategy supports this.

First, let's look at the destructive forces of worry and uncertainty. Physically these emotions cause us to be less creative and certainly less productive. And in any disruptive situation, the way to get out is through new innovative ideas and processes. So negative emotions will perpetuate negative outcomes.

Positive emotions on the other hand, improve immunity, induce more excitement, support creative problem solving, and productivity... and a personal sense of purpose breeds positive emotions. Combine purpose with gamification and collaboration and you have the recipe for TOTAL AWESOMENESS!

So how do we do this?

The potential to manifest a goal that will affect the organization while improving personal sense of value and happiness yields hope... and hope is the fuel for purpose... which is cultivated from the process, not the result, of creating something bigger, better, or more satisfying.

Creating a better life through work, for example, would support a greater Purpose. If employees were actively involved in creating a better Culture for them to eventually go back to, an Ideal Work Environment where they would thrive and succeed in their jobs... and create fun and diversity in the process, avoiding obstacles like Lockdowns and isolation... they would have a Greater Purpose that all can connect to (reducing isolation) because they are working for the future, the bright future!

And what if they united to achieve this? people to gain purpose and excitement through creating an Ideal Work Environment in a culture THEY create. A bright future they will engineer in downtime to improve life, productivity and engagement when they go back to work. They become the architects of a better life for themselves and others. They are elevating their sense of value and creating innovations to solve problems, improve organizations, and achieve personal goals.

The game:

The creation of teams that compete in strategy and problem solving but unite for one greater workplace where teams and individuals share the spoils of the visible results.

Here is the strategy:

1.	Measurement of the current culture using the Culture Evolution OCEAN tool provides a culture benchmark.

2.	A survey with 2 questions should be circulated to all individuals with an anonymous reply... here are the questions:

    a.	If you were the CEO, what would you change or do in the organization?

    b.	What are your biggest frustrations working here?

This will provide an understanding of what the future will bring when people begin to design their own culture.

3.	The CEO reaches out in a Video (yes this is

important because it is more personal) to the people stating that he is looking for their help. Then pause. Immediately, some may think "oh no, salary reduction, voluntary dismissal..." but then continues to share that we are going to create X cross-departmental teams to create the ideal and successful company. And that the staff should nominate people to create these teams, keeping in mind that anyone is eligible no matter their position, and they should choose people they like and trust. People who have the best interest of the people and the company in their hearts.

4.	HR should coordinate, tabulate, and organize the effort.

5.	These people will have a meeting (either online or offline) to understand their roles. The CEO should be in this initial meeting in line with the 4 factors to establishing the bases for leading a work gamification initiative (in the Choosing the Leader Avatar Chapter).

6.	In this first meeting, the CEO, HR, and the Key influencers chosen WILL set Culture Goals based on the survey and the OCEAN culture benchmark.

7.	The first meeting will also include the creation of the schedule and milestones for the first part of the game applying elements from the chapter "Creating Game Mechanics to WIN". Part of the winning formula will include a preview to the survey outcome (from "2") and recommendation on what to focus on that would be accepted later.

8. A second meeting sets preliminary ideas for the game mechanics to make milestone achievement fun.

9. The CEO communicates highlights the top 5 issues from the survey that have been deemed relevant and doable to the entire organization noting the people will have an opportunity to address a few of these through this initiative.

10. The key influencers then recruit people from multiple departments to be a part of their team or "cell", have a meeting to determine the Ideal Work Environment (the ultimate goal), and the guiding principles and behaviors required to achieve the Ideal Work Environment. All employees should be in a cell and cells should not have more than 20 people. Since recruitment is virtual, HR may need to support it.

11. The cell leaders come together online to consolidate the ideas and streamline them into 5 to 8 guiding principles and the behaviors that support them... to create more connection and help everyone get through the pandemic in a positive way and ultimately create an ideal working environment in the future.

12. In a virtual setting, measurement of defined behaviors will not be so easy to observe in individuals so they must be separated to the collective behaviors of a team.

13. The cells meet online to determine some of the primary issues they would like to fix. The cell leaders ask for a vote of the various issues as the most important and send the results to the HR coordinators who consolidate the collective work and share results with management to identify the doable elements. Cell outcomes may need more than one meeting, and each virtual meeting should not take more than one hour.

14. When the outcomes are clear, this is presented to the CEO and the management team (it is important the CEO is personally involved in this to inspire the value placed on it) on an online company meeting where everyone joins. **The guiding principles ARE ACCEPTED,** and Senior management chose one or two of the survey related initiative ideas they can work with and accept. Remember that this was already identified in the beginning and recommended to the key influencers, so these are not too much of a surprise. Plus, there were 5 highlighted and they can focus on 1 or 2. Because of the more virtual situation, it is essential to be more focused on 1 or 2 rather than all 5.

15. The implementation game mechanics (see the chapter "Creating Game Mechanics to WIN") are created with the senior management and key Influencers based on the outcome of the company meeting.

16. Milestones and definitions for team behaviors for created together with senior management. Game parameters for defined issues and problem-solving are established.

17. HR communicates the Milestones, Rules of the Game to everyone.

18. Unlike the physical implementation, each "Key influencer" cell will compete against the others in achieving clearly defined objectives and exhibiting team behaviors.

19. HR becomes the Game Master and is active in measurement of milestones and cell behaviors and communicating the results weekly. Squadli is used for cell behavior measurement.

20. Progress of culture evolution visualized in the OCEAN system comparison is communicated to maintain and grow motivation

21. Cell Behavior-based points are reset at the end of each month to support other cells to have an opportunity to rank and excel.

22.   Each milestone is a celebration and award event where teams, people and results are celebrated... this may only take 40 minutes but will have a HUGE impact.

23.   Award certificates are sent in advance to recipients and are shown when received along with a virtual handshake (like a real hand going into the camera... have fun with it)

24.   Measure the Culture Evolution and compare until culture goals are met.

25.   Then start over with a new set of influencers and new things to fix.

This process will require 3 to 4 hours a week online, but the connection, innovation, and productivity yielded from this initiative will far outweigh the extra time spent.

I remember my first time when I got to speak to senior management as a young employee, it was a meeting to rebrand the organization and I was part of a team that was invited to brainstorm. Even though the company was small, having the CEO listen to me, even in a group, was a big deal, that one meeting energized me for months. I felt that I mattered. And when a part of my idea was used, I was ecstatic and the company, its brand, and its goals were top of mind... for about 2 months at least... there wasn't any follow up or other opportunities to be heard. And there was no indication of how the rebranding I was a part of affected the outcome of the organization... so my excitement eventually died down.

In a virtual context, communication about HOW things are going and HOW we, the team are contributing to any improvements, no matter how small, is even more important than in live situations. Why… because we cannot see them, even the small little wins we may get a sense of achievement from are invisible if not regularly communication so daily communication and how close we are to simple milestones or any positive event from our efforts MEANS SOMETHING!

Direct communication from the leaders especially the CEO is essential. The more personal it gets the better (ok, I guess there are limits) like the CEO addressing you from his/her home and introducing you to the spouse of kids.

In a new normal it's not the virus that is our biggest danger, it is our emotions. We coop, we deal and some of us even thrive… but many still feel loss. Hope, fun, and connection are the keys to paving a brighter more successful future for people as well as organizations. Gamification is a tool, a strategy, and a beacon for humanity and business to flourish. As a leader, a more successful culture begins with two words… GAME ON!

Citations

Bethune S, Bossolo L. APA Survey Finds Feeling Valued at Work Linked to Well-Being and Performance. [Online] 2020 [cited] 2012 March 8.

Carmazzi AF and Sittiprapaporn P. Genetic Foundations of the Brain's Clarity Getting "Ambiguity Relief" Processes and Their Implications on Communication and Synergy. NeuroReport

Katz, E. Remote Workforce NPS: The Most Important Metric You're Missing. [Online] 2020 [cited] 2017 March 2.

He Q, Turel O and Bechara A. Brain anatomy alterations associated with Social Networking Site (SNS) addiction. Sci Rep. 2017; 7: 45064. DOI: 10.1038/srep45064

Dixit Sanjeev Dr.. Book Plan C: Building and Sustaining a High-Performance Culture by Design in the Virtual World. Mumbai: Passionpreneur Publishing. 2019.

Carmazzi AF. Observation and Genetic Foundations of the Brain's Clarity Achieving "Ambiguity Relief" Processes. Int. J. Adv. Res. 5(9): 1129-1140.

International Journal of Advanced Research 2017; 5:

www.ingramcontent.com/pod-product-compliance
Lightning Source LLC
Chambersburg PA
CBHW070539220526
45467CB00003B/995